Praise for *Through Old Ground*

"Randy Cross belongs to a species nearly extinct: the storyteller whose voice makes the Old Times dance again."
— Howard Bahr, author of *The Black Flower*

"Randy Cross's memoir *Through Old Ground* reads like a novel built around a series of events Cross experienced while growing up in St. Joseph, Tennessee, teaching English as a Fulbright Scholar in Rio de Janeiro, and later during his life in North Alabama. He plows through the 'old ground' of his memory to bring delightful incidents to the reader. His is a life built around love, adventure, and family. At no time does Cross lose sight of the importance of family from his childhood days in elementary school through the days in Brazil while teaching English, when his mother, who refuses to miss any happening, insists on seeing a murdered man in the street before she goes shopping. Here are poignant, honest, wise stories that vividly depict a by-gone era. It has beautiful moments, tied together with delightful comparisons. Cross offers some great belly-laugh stories, as well as overall laugh-out-loud stories. *Through Old Ground* and its charming stories will stay with the reader long after he has laid the book aside."
— Laura Hunter, author of *Beloved Mother*

"When I glanced at the title of this book, and the author's impressive credentials, I had no idea what to expect. It didn't take long for me to figure it out. In fact, I soon felt as if Dr. Cross had reached into my past, took hold of my memories, mixed them with his own recollections, and then fashioned them into these funny, inspiring, emotional tales. One of my favorites was 'Angels Unawares.' The description of the lightning storm immediately evoked one of my own best-loved childhood memories. Many of the stories affected me that way. I swan, it was like going home to Mama's house—front porch to be exact—one of the best places in the world. One of the best times. Thank you for the trip, Dr. Cross."
— Ann Swann, author of *Stutter Creek*

"*Through Old Ground* is an absolute treasure, a literary feast of personal stories from a Southern boy who traveled far and wide from his native Tennessee yet always carried the old homeplace in his heart. In these essays, the memory of growing up in a small town populated with colorful characters and a language of its own is treated every bit as lovingly as the eye-opening travels to exotic lands. This is a book that will make you laugh out loud on one page and blink back tears the next. Thank you, Dr. Randy Cross, for such a delightful read."

— Cassandra King, author of *Tell Me a Story:*
My Life with Pat Conroy

As much as the heartwarming memoir *Through Old Ground* is about its subject, it is also about those he loves and cares about most.
… In a loud, clear, and often hilarious voice, Randy Cross brings the American South to life in the twenty-four short vignettes that make up his memoir, *Through Old Ground*.
Written as a series of anecdotes shared in chronological order, Cross's memoir tracks his life from childhood through his time with the National Guard, into academia and beyond. Each anecdote is spotted with old-fashioned wisdom and platitudes passed down from his kinsfolk. And while at times its rants against changing cultural norms and shifts in language are wearying, the book is more often flushed with goodwill and a positive outlook.
Cross, a small-town Tennessee native born into a supportive but cantankerous family and raised to love language, traveled far and wide with the National Guard and as a Fulbright scholar. Family remained central to his life, and these stories hold a special place for his no-nonsense mother, who is seen haranguing a salesman about a faulty microwave and trailing Cross to the scene of a murder in Brazil.
Cross, meanwhile, is vivified by his snide sense of humor, his love of teaching language, and his affection for his hometown.
His is a story of a quiet life—one led without much adversity

and filled with the privileges of support and success. He recalls its events with the flavor of a storyteller regaling listeners on a porch, reminiscing on his more adventurous past—and sometimes going on.

Capturing formative moments, the memoir *Through Old Ground* delights in recalling warm and bizarre situations for the entertainment of others.

--Clarion Review
3 Stars

Twice a Fulbright Scholar, Ph.D. in English, Pulitzer Prize Nominee, College Professor, Musician, Author, World Traveler. All of these describe the remarkable Randy Cross. And there's at least one more: Actor. He performs to perfection the role of a lawyer in a small Southern town as depicted in *The Store*, a novel for which its author, T.S. Stribling, won the Pulitzer in 1933. Through all of his accomplishments and accolades, Randy Cross credits his childhood and growing-up years on the old ground that nurtured him in the little town of St. Joseph, Tennessee. This book, *Through Old Ground*, chronicles perfectly that part of Randy's fascinating autobiography.

--Billy Warren, City Historian
Florence Alabama

Through Old Ground

Randy Cross

Library of Congress Control Number: 2023942378
ISBN: 978-1-958273-79-1 Paperback
ISBN: 978-1-958273-78-4 Hardback
ISBN: 978-1-958273-80-7 eBook

Managing Editor — Angela Broyles
Interior Design — Katie Warren
Cover Design and Illustrations — Brooke P. Alexander

This book is dedicated to the memory of my dear
parents, Johnny and Marie Cross. They were
the center of my universe.

— Ran

"If you don't have a sense of humor, borrow or steal one from someone who does. It will come in handy when reason and anger and justice fail."

— Randy Cross

Table of Contents

Foreword

Randy Cross has given us a lovely and heartfelt remembrance of a boyhood spent in the rural South—and values rooted in "old ground" that he carried with him through a long career in teaching.

Cross spent much of that time at Calhoun Community College in Alabama, but not until after various forays of cautious adventure as a Fulbright Scholar in Portugal and Brazil. He remembers a trip to the Amazon jungle, the red eyes of alligators glowing in the dark, and a tarantula that made its way inside the mosquito netting of his hammock.

Cross shares such tales with wry good humor, but it is clear in the telling that the adrenaline rush was not his style. He was more content traveling to Wales with his wife, Kim, searching on a whim for the grave of Richard Llewelyn, the author of their favorite novel, *How Green Was My Valley*. They carried with them a handwritten note: "God bless you, Richard Llewelyn, wherever you are."

Cross was an English teacher by trade, a lover of literature and good grammar who sought to impart those passions to his students. At first glance, it might seem an improbable profession for a boy who had worked side by side with his father, plowing dark, fertile fields behind a rented mule. But Cross makes it clear that it was not.

In graceful prose and easygoing stories, he recaptures the quiet strength of his raising. Life was centered on the soil and the bonds of family—and also the church, a source of multiple prohibitions, including the gateway sin of dancing. But in Cross's case there was more. He recounts a trip to a hardware store with his father, where a tattered old man outside was selling pencils for a quarter. Randy didn't notice him at first, but his father saw the chance for a Bible lesson. He placed some bills in the old man's hand, and when they were out of earshot, he quoted gently from Matthew 25:40: "Verily I say unto you, inasmuch as ye have done it unto one of the least of these my brethren, ye have done it unto me."

These were durable lessons for a boy to carry forward into life, and Cross remembers them fondly. As with Andy Griffith's Mayberry or Harper Lee's Maycomb, the recognition we feel may carry the aura of idealized truth. But in a time of American culture wars, which all too often bring out the worst, Cross quietly celebrates the best.

I am grateful for this fine book.

—Frye Gaillard, Writer in Residence,
University of South Alabama

Mama and the Microwave Oven

When microwave ovens first appeared, Mama decided we needed one.

"If other people can have things, so can we," she said. We drove to an appliance store up in Lawrenceburg and found exactly what she wanted: an Amana Radar Range, four hundred and seventy-five dollars. When the store manager approached, Mama said: "Yes sir. I want to buy one of these microwave ovens, but not this display model. Do y'all have one still in the box? I do not want a demonstrator."

The microwave on display was the only one he had left the manager said, but he assured us it had never been turned on. "It ain't never even been plugged in," he said.

Mama paid cash, and a clerk loaded it in the car. We could not wait to get home and watch it boil water in a Styrofoam cup and fry bacon on a paper towel. Like two children on Christmas morning, we placed it on the counter, plugged it in, and put the cup of water inside. We set the timer and punched it on. Every light in the house went out. We replaced the blown fuse and tried again with the same result.

Then Mama opened the microwave door and examined the inside with a flashlight. "Well, would you look at that? He lied to me. There's grease all over the top and sides of this thing. You get this oven loaded back in that car."

Half an hour later, the manager met us in the aisle. I sat the oven down and waited. He could do the right thing, apologize and return Mama's money, or he could assume that she was a frail, spineless woman from the country accustomed to taking "no" for an answer.

"I want my money back," Mama said. "You told me this oven had never been used. The whole insides is covered with grease. The only thing it'll cook is fuses."

I stopped breathing and waited. Would he be smart and refund her money, or would he crawl inside that volcano on the brink of eruption? He jumped in with both feet.

"We don't give refunds. That's store policy. We can repair this one for you."

I wanted to intervene, to warn him, but the first stream of lava had already begun to ooze over the brim. Besides, I wasn't on safe ground either, so I stepped back to watch. After all, I had not pushed him. He had jumped—voluntarily—so I decided to let him burn.

Mama took charge. "Well, I'm gonna tell you two things. One, you're gonna change your store policy today. Two, you're giving me my money back 'cause I ain't leaving without it."

"I've already told you once," he said, jabbing his finger in her face. "You're not getting your money back. You can forget that."

I saw the explosion and retreated another step. He just stood there like a fool.

Finally, the glare from Mama's eyes scorched him until he said, "I'll tell you what I will do. I've got a new shipment of these ovens coming in next week, and I'm going to send a truck to your house and have one of my men install you a new oven."

"Good," Mama said. "I want you to. Send him on, and when he drives up to my house, I'm gonna have Sheriff Davis arrest him for trespassing. Then I'm going run your truck into the gully at the end of my driveway and pour gas on it, set it on fire and burn it up, and sue you for trashing up my ditch." Mama's wrath engulfed the store.

"Everybody!" Mama yelled at the dozen other customers nearby. "Y'all come here. I want to tell you something." They gathered around like children at a schoolground fight. "You see this man here? He lies like a dog. He sold me an old used microwave oven for a new one, and if you're smart, you'll go anywhere else and buy what you want or do without."

The manager attempted to speak.

"You hush," Mama said, "I ain't through with you yet. Do you know Bob Olsen?"

"No."

"Well, you gonna know him. He's that man on the Channel Four News—WSM out of Nashville—that goes around and films trash like you who tries to beat poor old people out of their hard-earned money. And when that Channel Four truck rolls in here and he broadcasts all over middle Tennessee on the six o'clock news what a lying, cheating dog you are, then I guess you'll know him."

The manager squirmed around to his cashier. "Write her a check for four-hundred and seventy-five dollars plus tax."

"I'll not be taking a check from you," Mama said. "It wouldn't be no better than your word. You're giving me cash." The manager himself counted out the bills into Mama's hand.

Several of the other former customers applauded and then followed us down the aisle past that greasy, fuse-cooking microwave oven taking their business somewhere else or doing without. Mama and I laughed all the way home.

The Appleton Sisters

When I was old enough to know where my sisters spent their days, I wanted to go to school, too. They came home with tales of reading and writing, recess, and eating lunch in the cafeteria where Aunt Annie cooked. I felt punished because I couldn't go with them, and I counted the years until I was six and could have my own paper, pencils, book satchel, and stories. Kindergarten and preschool had not made their way to the country, nor had any of the other halfway houses common today. When we were six, we started to school, the first grade.

Only then did we learn our ABCs, how to read, and how to write our names. Parents did not teach their children those things at home. At least mine didn't, and I don't believe I was the exception. As a result, Miss Mary Belle Appleton, the primary teacher, met a new group of six-year-old ignorant, illiterate children every first day of school.

The summer I turned six, Mama bought me a big round pencil and an oblong notebook with the letters of the alphabet on the front cover. Alternating solid and dotted pale blue lines on the newsprint pages prescribed the height of each capital and lowercase letter I would learn to make. Grandest of all was a brown book satchel adorned with a drawing of Red Ryder astride his rearing horse, Thunder, accompanied by a pair of brown jersey gloves, the picture duplicated on their red-fringed cuffs. My eagerness intensified. I was ready for school.

On the first day of classes, Mother held my gloved hand as we entered the St. Joseph Elementary School. I carried my book satchel with the other. In the foyer, two things etched themselves into my memory: the smell of the freshly oiled floor and the huge four-leaf clover flag of the 4-H club mounted on the wall. Beneath it, within easy reach, a fire axe rested on two hooks. No one ever touched it during my eight years at that school, or ever considered touching it, or even thought about considering touching it. It was not allowed.

The principal, Mr. Abercrombie, patrolled the halls and the playground carrying a barber's leather strap. He and his strap kept us within the school grounds, kept us silent as we stood in line for the water fountain, lunch, or an assembly program in the gym, and kept our minds—let alone our hands—off the axe. He was never cruel nor harsh, not even with the big, barefooted farm boys from Mt. Nebo—or over on the Iron City Road—who loved to fight at recess. He always smiled as he lashed the transgressors on the playground. The school was his domain, and I never knew a man, not even in the Army, so comprehensively in charge as Mr. Curtis Abercrombie.

I had seen Miss Mary Belle Appleton when I accompanied Mama to PTA meetings or school plays my sisters were in, but I had never met her until that morning. She stood in the door of her classroom, her gray hair cut short, wearing a pink flowery dress. She smelled like Mrs. Johnson, the Avon Lady who came to our house each month and from whom Mama always made us hide when we were sure she hadn't seen us through the window. "I got enough Avon now to float a battleship," she would say as we ran to the back of the house or ducked down behind the couch.

"Miss Mary Belle, this is Randy," Mother said. Without warning, all my ambitions for an education evaporated. Nothing, not my sisters' stories, my Red Ryder book satchel and gloves, not even the axe on the wall, held any allure for me. I jerked my hand out of Mama's and fled down the oily hall, out the door, and climbed back into our green Ford.

A minute later, Mother opened the car door. "Come on back in, honey; it's time to take up books."

As Mama apologized to Miss Mary Belle for my behavior, I broke loose again, ran out of the building, jumped in the car, and locked all four doors.

Seconds later, Mother was pulling at the handle.

"You open this door right now," she said.

The only way to deal with Mama was through immediate and unconditional surrender. I opened the door and got out. Mama dragged me up the hall and passed me off to Miss Mary Belle like a baton in a relay race. Then she was gone.

I tried to escape, but Miss Mary Belle grabbed me by the shoulders, spun me around, shook me, and shoved me through the door. Pointing to the others staring quietly up at me, she said: "What if everybody acted like you?" She didn't wait for an answer. Pushing me in front of her, she guided me to a little red cane-bottomed chair and chunked me down in it. I was still wearing my gloves.

"I want to quit school," I said, snubbing.

"You can't quit school," she said. "You can't ever quit school. Now sit still and hush."

I don't recall a lesson I ever learned so quickly: Miss Mary Belle would have her way. She did not provide alternatives, allow choices, consider wishes, nor equivocate. If we misbehaved, she paddled us right there in the classroom, in front of everybody, or, for minor offenses, she threw an eraser from the blackboard and hit us in the head. A rectangular-shaped patch of chalk dust in our hair was a badge of honor we wore proudly the remainder of the day. Only before going home would we brush it away to keep our parents from seeing it.

Miss Mary Belle Appleton acquired her values and ethics from a vanished time and dispensed them generously, unselfishly, on us. Her philosophy of education was simple: the teacher told the students what to do, and they did it. If we failed to obey, she punished us immediately. Still, if we were hurt on the playground, she doctored us just as quickly from a little green bottle of Campho-Phenique, which she used on everything from cuts to black eyes. I can still smell it.

As the months passed, she transformed us. We filled notebooks with our names, numbers, and with sentences we copied from books, always placing our index fingers between words for proper spacing. All the while, we were learning to read, first about Dick and Jane and their dog Spot that chased a red ball, and later about Tip and Mitten. We read aloud, and any time we missed words or hesitated too long between them, we stayed in at recess and read the passage again while Miss Mary Belle sat beside us. She missed recess, too. If we read without faltering, we joined our literate colleagues on the playground for softball, tag, or Red Rover until Mr. Ab appeared, strap in one hand, ringing a brass bell with the other. With the first clang, we stopped our play, ran and lined up at the front door. Once we stood quietly in place, we entered the sanctum without talking and tiptoed down the dark hall.

I never ceased being afraid of Miss Mary Belle, but I grew to love her. All of us did, I think, and we were as eager to gain her favor as we were to avoid her scorn. If we read well, sometimes she almost smiled, her eyes and voice softened, and she touched us on the shoulder. "You did that well," she would say. "This time."

She taught us manners and etiquette, fair play, and courtesy. In the cafeteria, she walked behind us as we ate. "Billy Wilson," she said one day, "I've told you before. Don't hold your fork in your fist. Hold it in your fingers as though it were a pencil. A fork is a utensil, not a weapon."

"Yes, ma'am," Billy said, embarrassed, his voice quivering. "But I don't know how to eat no other way. Thangs falls off my fork when I try to use it like you told me." We all froze. His response sounded like talking back, and we knew the consequences for that. Miss Mary Belle put her hand on Billy's shoulder, and her eyes smiled.

"Do you hold a fork that way at home?" she said softly.

"No, ma'am. We always just eat with spoons."

She bent down and hugged him. "You're a good boy, Billy," she said. "You may dust the erasers this afternoon."

Once I left the St. Joseph Elementary School, I did not see Miss Mary Belle for over twenty years. One Sunday afternoon, I was visiting my parents when I answered the phone. "Doctor Cross?"

"Yes, ma'am, Miss Mary Belle."

"I can't believe you recognized my voice. May I call you Randy?"

"Yes, ma'am, please do."

She gave me my first invitation ever to have tea.

When I arrived, she was standing in the door, waiting. We sat in her parlor and talked. "The day I put you that little red chair, did you think you would ever finish graduate school and become Doctor Cross?"

"No, ma'am," I said. "I didn't think I'd ever finish the first grade." She laughed out loud. I never knew she could.

Still smelling like Mrs. Johnson, she hugged me as I left her house. "You are a good boy," she said. "Please come back and see me when you can." I promised her I would, but I was teaching in Brazil when she died.

She had been right all those years before. I couldn't quit school. I couldn't ever quit. Since the day Red Ryder and I sat in the little chair in front of the class, I have been in school, either as a student or as a teacher.

Miss Mary Belle Appleton introduced me to a

world of learning, a world of wonder. She taught me to read and write and to respect those in authority. "What if everybody acted like you?" she had asked me that September morning over fifty years ago. It is still a good question.

***

Miss Mary Belle's sister, Miss Eula, taught fourth grade. I still owe her a deep debt of gratitude for changing my life when I was nine years old. Each day after lunch she read to us for half an hour, and she introduced us country children to Homer's *Iliad* and *The Odyssey*. Who could ever forget the one-eyed Cyclops? The same is true for Joel Chandler Harris's Uncle Remus who gave us Brer Rabbit and Brer Fox. He lay low. Miss Eula's accents delighted all us students and caused our laughter to echo down the hall.

Perhaps most important to me was her reading of Tom Sawyer and Huckleberry Finn. Years later at the University of Mississippi, I wrote my doctoral dissertation on Mark Twain and religion. This allowed me to earn two Fulbright Scholarships and teach at universities on three continents. Miss Eula opened class each day by reading us a passage from the Bible, a routine I have always remembered. I would never have accomplished my scholarly pursuits if not for Miss Eula's emphasis on literature and geography when I was a young boy at the St. Joseph Elementary School.

I saw my first globe of the world when I was in her class. About the size of a basketball, it sat mounted on her desk and was off limits to all of us students. Miss Eula knew that a spinning globe was too much of a temptation for us if she was in the room or not. Globe spinning by students was strictly forbidden. I realize now that Miss Eula's dictum was her way of stirring up our enthusiasm for the whirling ball of blue, pink, tan, green, and orange.

Geography was not a part of our fourth-grade curriculum the way English and math were, but Miss Eula had her unique way of incorporating it that made us love it. All fifteen of us looked forward to our geography class with eager anticipation, and we never knew when it was going to occur. She surprised us twice each week with the same announcement: "Okay boys and girls, it's visiting time." That was our cue to scurry to form a horseshoe circle around the front and sides of her desk. We always stood silent and waited for her to spread her hand over the North Pole and give the colorful globe a fast spin. All the colors formed a blurry kaleidoscope as the tiny turning world mesmerized us all.

Miss Eula closed her eyes as the globe spun and placed her right index finger at a random location as it slowed to a stop. Then, with eyes still closed, she put her finger down and brought the world to a stop and marked the day's lesson with her fingertip. If she touched an ocean, she pointed out the continents that bordered it. If her finger touched land, she talked about the country, history, and language.

I will always remember my favorite time we gathered around the spinning globe. As it slowed to a stop, Miss Eula pressed her finger on a narrow strip of land in Europe that jutted out into the North Atlantic Ocean. "This little country is Portugal, and its capital is Lisbon," she said. "Portugal and its neighboring country Spain form the Iberian Peninsula. Those who live in Spain speak Spanish, and the citizens of Portugal speak Portuguese, just as many do in South America and Africa.

"Portugal has produced many navigators and explorers, one of whom is the famous Vasco da Gama, the man who opened the Spice Routes from Europe to the Orient."

I had no idea what Spice Routes were, but I loved the way the words sounded. Miss Eula made us all repeat the phrase together: "Spice Routes." I still think they are pretty words.

Thirty years later, I stepped off the plane in Lisbon, Portugal, where I would spend the year teaching American Literature at the New University of Lisbon as a Fulbright Scholar. I had earned degrees from the University of North Alabama and a Ph.D. in English from the University of Mississippi.

After a few days of getting settled in, I visited the lovely Monastery of Jeronimos near the Tagus River. In the vestibule sat the sepulcher of Vasco da Gama. A stone carving of the great explorer lay atop his tomb, his hands pressed together in the pose of prayer. Stained glass windows that joined the ceiling and the walls allowed soft colors to drift among the venerable stones.

I knelt and placed my hands around those of Vasco da Gama. As tears filled my eyes, I looked up in wonder. "Oh Miss Eula," I said. "I am here."

Angels Unawares

L ate one stormy Friday night, Daddy was working the graveyard shift at the Reynolds Metals Company down in Sheffield, Alabama. He rode the Blue Bird work bus, and it usually got him home shortly after one o'clock in the morning. My sisters Deanna and Vicki and I were in Mama's bed with her. Rain beat on the aluminum siding, thunder boomed and shook the windows, and lightning ripped and spewed across the sky. We were not afraid. When it came up a cloud, Mama gathered all the pillows in the house and built a fortress around the top of the bed. "Don't worry now," Mama would say. "Lightning can't strike through feathers. Chickens don't ever get struck."

Mama recited and read poems to us during storms to occupy our minds. One was "Song of Hiawatha," and another was "Somebody's Mother" by Mary Dow Brine, which always made her cry. She had just started:

> The woman was old and ragged and gray
> And bent with the chill of the Winter's day.

And then we heard the pounding, louder than the storm, the side of a fist hammering on the front door.

"Listen!" Mama whispered out loud. "Everybody be real quiet." The knocking continued while we slipped out of bed, tiptoed to the living room, and Mama eased up a slat on the Venetian blind just enough to see out.

"Open the door, Marie," a man yelled. "I need to talk to you."

"Law," Mama said, "that's Bluford Bradley. What we gonna do? You know he always carries guns wherever he goes, and I'm afraid of 'em. Besides, your daddy won't be home for hours."

***

Whenever Bluford came into town, he often arrived standing on his wooden field slide drawn by his horse, Chester. Most men in our town built such a device to help with their farming. It was made of wood, including the runners and the frame. Usually around four feet wide and six feet long, the slide carried a variety of plows and tools the farmer needed during the day. Bluford used his slide for transportation into town. Those of us sitting on Mr. Green's store porch, just across the road from our house, could hear the sound of the wooden runners as they scraped on the tar and gravel pavement. What a racket it made along with the clicking and clacking of Chester's steel shoes. Bluford always brought his rifle, which he propped in the corner where the front and side rails met. His big country dog Old Rock sat beside Bluford where he stood holding the reins. We loved to hear Bluford yell out, "Hold on, Old Rock, we're going through town."

Our greatest thrill came when Bluford stopped at the store and took a seat on the porch bench. He drew his pistol and shot walnuts off the tree in our front yard. All of us boys liked and admired him so much. He was the only man we knew who went armed, a pistol always strapped to his waist, the tip of the holster bound to his thigh with a thin strip of leather.

***

The storm continued to howl. "Open the door, Mama. He won't hurt us. He's gonna get lightning struck out there," I said. There was a long pause.

"Y'all stand right here," Mama said, the strength back in her voice.

She turned the deadbolt and opened the door. The rain poured off the brim of Bluford's hat, his overcoat sopping wet.

"What is it, Bluford?"

"Marie, I'm sorry to bother y'all, but I need you to drive me up to Lawrenceburg. That boy of mine is in the hospital, and my car won't crank. I need to go see about him."

"Law, Bluford, Johnny's working, and it's just me and the kids here. I'm afraid to be out at night."

Bluford pulled back the right side of his soggy coat and draped it behind the grip of his holstered revolver. As he patted the pistol, he said, "You ain't got nothing to be afraid of with me. This little angel will take care of you. I can promise you that."

Mama's eyes froze on the gun. "Go see if Reb Farris or Bill Springer, one of the men, will take you. I don't want to get the children out, and I can't leave them here in this storm." And then softly, "What's wrong with your son?"

"All I know is he's had a spell and they've took him to the hospital. He's got the sugar bad."

I was ready to go, and so were Deanna and Vicki, and Mama knew it. Lightning crackled, and thunder roared up from down around the Mule Barn.

"Come on in a minute, Bluford, while we get ready," Mama said.

"I'll wait for y'all out here. I don't want to mess up your floor."

The five of us ran down to the garage in the rain to our 1957 persimmon and peach Mercury Montclair with a big gold "M" centered on the grill. That's what we called it: The Big M. Deedy and Vick got in the back seat, Mama drove, and I sat between her and Bluford and the angel on his hip. When I asked him if his gun was loaded, he didn't answer. He laughed, placed his hand on my knee, squeezed it a few times, and said, "This is how a horse eats corn."

Mama told me to hush and help her watch the road.

We let Bluford out at the hospital half an hour later. "I won't never forget this," he said.

The storm lifted by the time we got back to St. Joseph. Lightning stopped ripping open the sky and instead illuminated it every few minutes in soft winking sheets off to the east. Thunder drifted over the miles in comforting rumbles, like friendly artillery.

"Home again, home again, jiggidy jog," Mama said as we pulled into the garage. It was nearly midnight. Daddy would be home by one. "Are y'all sleepy?" Mama said. Nobody was. "Let's stay up and wait for your daddy. He's out in the storm, too, on that old work bus."

When Daddy came home, we told him all about our adventure. Mama had softened up on Bluford some, but she talked about the gun and how it scared her to death when she first saw it.

"Bluford's had a hard old time all his life," Daddy said. "I don't believe he'd ever hurt another soul. Let's go to bed now and remember this: Sometimes when we do right, we might be entertaining angels unawares."

Mama turned to us children. "Sleep tight," she said, "and don't let the June bugs bite."

I Miss My Language

English is a second language for me, at least the English taught in classrooms. I grew up with a far different language, more colorful, more expressive, and a hundred times more comfortable than the one shaped to fit neatly on the pages of a grammar book.

I always enjoyed Miss McDonald's visits to our house when I was a boy. I liked her and the way she talked. She did not actually participate in conversations; she merely responded with expressions that flowed from her with ease.

If someone said, "Ain't it hot?" she'd respond with "I'm a'tellin' you. Ain't that the truth?" If the other person said, "They say the school bus run off of the road this morning and a bunch of students got hurt," she'd say, "I dis declare to my time." Or "Don't that beat all?" or "I'll swan."

Once another woman who was visiting said, "I picked enough sallet this morning for two messes."

"That's a right smart," Miss McDonald said.

"Yeah, I done looked both messes and got one on to cook."

"I'll swanee," Miss McDonald said. "Lawzy mercy."

That good woman had so mastered the English language that a few expressions carried her safely across any topic that arose.

Other people whose world I once inhabited made language work well for them, too. Unlike Miss McDonald, Clinton Roberson, who had traveled with the fair, could talk for hours without pausing. On Raleigh Green's store porch, he taught me about stream of consciousness years before I studied William Faulkner in college.

When Clinton finished one tale, he'd head into another one on the same breath. "Imo tell y'all a story right now you might not b'lieve, but I swear it's so. Hit would take too long to put in all the details, but I won't leave out none of the good parts. You'ns listen good 'cause I'm fixin' to run through this like green apples through the hired girl.

"When I was in show biness, we was working a fair just this side of Knoxville. I was running the Tilt-a-Whirl and fell in with a little gal working the dance stage just down the midway. She was from Ill-a-noise. She liked the Tilt-a-Whirl good, so she'd come and see me between acts, and I'd let her ride free—put her on a car by herself. Ever time she swung by, I'd hit the speed button a time or two to slang her to one side and make her come back around quicker. One day it rained out the crowd and cleared the midway. We was suppose to shut down when that happened, but here she come just the same, like a old wet hen totin' her shoes. Y'all ever seen red painted toenails on muddy feet? I hadn't neither till that day. Oh my, I'ma tellin' you." And on he would go.

Clinton's stories most always dealt in romance. The men and boys on the store porch traveled mainly behind mules and middle buster plows down corn and cotton rows. Thus, as he talked, we sat enthralled, silent, maybe pondering faraway places like Knoxville, show business, or rain-soaked Yankee girls with muddy red toenails. What a lovely world we lived in.

I am convinced that my interest in language came from the small Southern town where I grew up. It was a linguistic goldmine from which its citizens shoveled out provincial speech in great, unpolished clods.

I miss my first language—the one I learned in St. Joseph, Tennessee—but I am forced to make do with the one that has, over the years, taken its place. I am an English teacher by trade, a beautiful irony.

One semester, a girl in my literature class pointed out something in a Robert Frost poem I had never considered. "What an extraordinary insight," I told her. "Your interpretation of that line elucidates the entire passage."

Miss McDonald could have said it much better and succinctly: "I'll dis declare to my time." And while I do hold a Ph.D. in English from the University of Mississippi itself, I often resort to the language I learned in St. Joe when I was a boy. A few weeks ago, I was rummaging through a kitchen cabinet, slamming its doors, and jerking open drawers in search for a bottle of aspirin. My wife Kim was sitting in our office and heard the racket. "What on earth are you doing?" she asked.

"Ize a-huntin' uh asburn," I told her.

"Well, Doctor Cross," she said, laughing, "do you realize that every word in that sentence you just spoke is wrong?" I paused, thought for a moment, and realized she was correct.

"Did you understand what I was saying?"

"Yes," she said. "I was hunting an aspirin."

"Well, if you understood it, it must have been a good sentence. After all, you know that I speak multiple languages. That sentence was from the first one I ever learned." Oh, how I miss my language.

Lester Flatt and Earl Scruggs

Years ago, I went to the mall looking for a portion of my youth that I had allowed to lie dormant for too long. Standing outside of the record shop, I braced myself for the selections the high school-age employees would be playing too loudly on the store's stereo system and walked inside, ready for defeat. After hearing my request with a puzzled look, the smiling young man escorted me to a rack and thumbed through a stack of CDs. "Here it is," he said: "Flatt and Scruggs Live at Vanderbilt University."

Back at home, I loaded the CD into the player and smiled as the familiar baritone voice of the announcer, T. Tommy Cutrer, said: "I've known these boys and worked with them for seven years now on radio and television." Boys. Lester Flatt, Earl Scruggs, and the Foggy Mountain Boys.

I am unable to stretch my memory back far enough to lose them. They are engrained with Washington and Lincoln in my mind, but I have their voices, their music to illuminate their fedoras, Earl's sparkling banjo, and Lester's big Martin guitar.

My father, a fine musician, saw to it that his children grew up surrounded by a variety of music:

guitar, fiddle, mandolin, banjo, anything that was broadcast over Nashville's WSM, the clear channel voice of the Grand Ole Opry. I thought the entire world woke up each morning in time to hear Lester and Earl's 5:45 live broadcast sponsored by Martha White flour. Goodness gracious good and light Martha White.

As much a part of the show as Uncle Josh's whining dobro guitar was the smooth voice of T. Tommy introducing the first number, usually a rousing bluegrass tune that galloped along at the insistence of Earl Scruggs' banjo virtuoso. And then, the voice of Lester Flatt himself: "A spayshul great big howdy to ye," and they would ease into "Cabin on the Hill" or "You are my Flower," our favorite. "Y'all listen," Daddy would say. "They don't miss a lick."

One Thursday night in 1958 when I was seven, they performed at the St. Joseph Elementary School, where I was in the second grade. I sat rapt throughout the show as I listened to the songs I knew by heart. By this time, they had a weekly television show out of Nashville, 6:00 p.m. on Saturday. We never missed it. I saw them in color for the first time that night in the school gymnasium. Lester and Earl wore red bow ties. Half an hour into the show, Earl exchanged his banjo for the guitar, they took off their hats, and sang "Paul and Silas" and "Just a Little Walk With Jesus." We knew not to clap for those.

When I was in college in the early 1970s, I played guitar and sang with a folk music group. We somehow were given the honor of fronting for Lester Flatt and Earl Scruggs and the Foggy Mountain Boys when they played a concert at the university. They stood just off stage and listened while we performed. I had never been more nervous nor missed as many notes. As our group left the stage, Lester stopped us. "That was some mighty fine music y'all were playing," he said. I thought I was going to die. Perhaps he never forgot their audition for Bill Monroe.

The CD I purchased was recorded in 1963 when I was thirteen, the year before Daddy bought me a 1952 Martin D-18 guitar. It is the finest instrument I have ever held in my hands. I can only imagine the music it must be capable of producing. I play mostly at home with a small group of friends who love the old songs as I do. And while I have never surpassed mediocrity as a musician, I have discovered since listening again to the Foggy Mountain Boys the style that for years I have attempted to emulate: Lester Flatt's fluid guitar runs and the syncopations that float up from Uncle Josh's dobro and Earl Scruggs' banjo and guitar.

Still the album is much more than the faultless renditions of good music. It is a pipeline to my past, a period of profound influences and the charmed days of youth. I am now past middle age, Lester Flatt and

Earl Scruggs have been gone for years, and the Foggy Mountain Boys have long since played their last song together. Only Martha White has stayed the same. My memory conjures her small hands clasping her smiling face. But the music remains as fresh and inspiring as I remember from their early morning radio show decades ago. If you don't believe me, just listen to the Boys, "the masters," as T. Tommy called them, as they play live from Vanderbilt. They don't miss a lick.

Sunday Snow

My daddy was not a pulpit preacher, but his life was a series of sermons. His words, his actions, and his kind heart were examples of goodness to all who knew him.

I was fourteen years old when Mother, Daddy, and I woke up one winter Sunday morning with a beautiful two-inch snow covering the ground. As Mama began to prepare breakfast, the telephone rang. The caller was a man from church letting us know that our worship service had been cancelled because of the weather. Daddy said he understood that decision because some of the people in our Southern town were not accustomed to driving on frozen roads.

After breakfast, Daddy asked me to get the broom and go outside with him. At the end of the driveway near the barn sat our old blue Chevrolet pickup truck covered with two inches of snow the night had brought. Daddy swept off the windshield and windows, the headlights and the taillights. Then he knelt down by a rear tire and began letting out the air. Once it was half flat, he performed the same operation on the other rear tire. I asked why he was doing that. "This will make the tires wider, and they will be less likely to spin," he said.

A few feet away was a stack of stove wood. We began picking it up and placing it in the bed of the truck directly above the half-inflated tires. "This wood will create weight on the back axle and increase the traction a great deal. We shouldn't have any trouble on the road."

"Won't this damage the deflated tires?" I asked.

"No," Daddy said, "this two inches of snow will make a fine cushion between the rubber and the asphalt."

After starting the engine and turning on the heater, we went back to the house to get Mother. She was ready to go, so we all climbed into the cab of the truck—Daddy driving, Mama on the passenger side, and me in the middle. We eased down the hill from our house onto the road that led to church, a trip of about two miles. There were no tire tracks in the snow, so we knew we were the first to be driving on that part of the road. We had a grand time easing slowly through our little town and looking at the beauty the snow had created.

When we arrived at the church, we were the only people there. Daddy let us in with his key. The three of us walked down the center aisle and formed a triangle near the altar. Mother and I stood next to each other, and Daddy faced us. "Let's bow our heads and begin with a prayer," he said. Then we sang a song. Following that, Daddy asked me to read from the Bible, and I chose one of my favorite passages, the first five verses of Genesis. Then we sang again. Next came communion with prayers of thanks. We sang the final song, and Daddy led us in the closing prayer. Then he quoted these words from Jesus: "For where two or three are gathered together in my name, there am I in the midst of them" (Matthew 18:20).

Immediately following his recitation, he said, "All right, let's go home now." And we did, riding through the same marvelous wonderland that had taken us to an experience I will never forget.

"Train up a child in the way he should go: and when he is old, he will not depart from it" (Proverbs 22:6).

Billy and Linda Mae

Billy Tidwell lived across the L&N railroad track from us at the top of a little hill. He was, in the parlance of that time, a cool cat. He wore a tight white T-shirt with a pack of cigarettes wrapped in the left sleeve. His snug blue jeans completed his ensemble except for the item that caused every boy in town to envy him: a pair of black loafers with white lightning streaks down the sides. Steel taps covered half the heels of each shoe. We could hear him coming by the sounds of clacking and scraping on the tar and gravel road. He always had his hair Lucky Tigered back into a black duck tail.

Billy and my sister Deanna—eight years older than me—were good friends, just buddies who had grown up together in St. Joseph, Tennessee. Billy came to visit her often, and they would sit in the porch swing and laugh and talk. Although I was just a young boy, I loved hearing their conversations while I sat on the porch steps.

Another reason Billy visited often was because he was struck on Linda Mae Quillen, one of Deanna's best friends who also spent a lot of time in our porch swing. I will always remember one particular day when Billy and Deanna were talking and swinging. "Deedy," Billy said. "I sure would like to go out with Linda Mae, but I don't know how to go about it."

"Just ask her, Billy," Deanna said.

"I can't. Whenever I try to talk to her I get nervous. My throat tightens up and my mouth gets dry. Whatever I try to say comes out shaky. I couldn't blame her for not wanting to go out with somebody like me."

"Oh, Billy," my sister said. "You don't have to be afraid to talk to Linda Mae. She has a sweet heart and wouldn't ever hurt your feelings. Here's what you need to know to fix all of this. Girls love to be complimented. Linda Mae is coming home with me from school tomorrow, and I'll make sure we are sitting here in the swing by three-thirty. You come strolling down the hill like you're going to Mr. Green's store. When you get almost there, I'll call for you to come over and visit with us. Between now and tomorrow afternoon, you give it a lot of thought and come up with the sweetest, kindest compliment you can say to Linda Mae. Her reaction will let you know that you can ask her to go out with you."

"Okay, I'll do it," Billy said. "I'll see you tomorrow at three-thirty."

The next afternoon, the girls were in the swing just as Deanna promised. Little brother Randy was sitting on the steps. I wanted to see and hear how things came out and learn about romance.

Billy came right on time, scraping his heel taps on that old tar and gravel road. Just before he stepped up on Mr. Green's porch, Deanna called out "Hey, Billy, come here." Billy looked surprised.

Then he came easing across the road to our small front yard. He stood there for a long moment, and then he took three more steps toward the swing. He stopped, looked at the ground for a few seconds, and then he raised his head, looked at her and said, "Linda Mae, you tear me up like a new jar of kraut." She jumped out of the swing, ran into the house, and shut the door.

"Billy," Deanna said after the shock settled a bit, "you and I need to have a discussion about compliments."

"I did the best I could," he said, "and I thank you Deedy for trying to help me." Then he turned and eased across the road to the store and on to the railroad before he headed up the hill toward home.

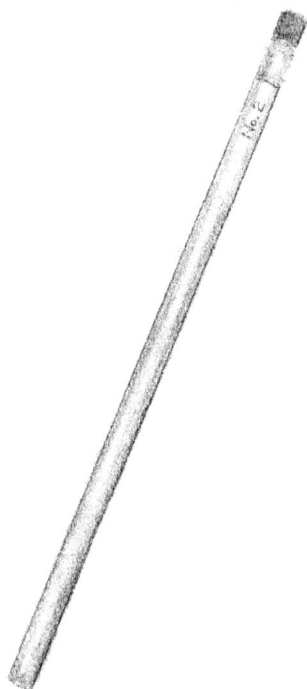

Squirter

On a Saturday morning around lunch time when I was about ten years old, I walked into our yard and found Daddy planting a flower bed near the outside faucet. "Hey, Ran," he said. "I've been looking for you to help me set out these pretty flowers for your mother."

"I'm sorry I wasn't here to help you, but I've been up at Ray's house helping him wash their new car. We had a good time using a gadget his daddy bought in Florence at K-Mart. You just screw it on the end of the hosepipe, turn the water on high, aim it at whatever you want to wash, and squeeze the handle on the squirter. The water comes spewing out and sends the dirt and mud flying. It's a great way to blast the tires and wheel wells. If you press the handle gently, the water comes out in a cone of soft water. It would be good for watering flowers and hosing down the mule after she has plowed all day. I think the squirter can really come in handy."

The next morning during breakfast, Daddy told me that we were going to take a little trip in the truck when we finished eating. We headed south and ended up half an hour later in the K-Mart parking lot. I was excited as we entered the vestibule, and I was anxious to enter the store's main sales areas. As I grasped the door handle, I felt Daddy's gentle hand pat me on the shoulder. I turned and looked him in the face. "Can't you see?" he asked. "Don't you know who is sitting there?"

"Yes, sir, I can see," I said.

"Well, you missed something you should have seen. Walk with me over to the corner."

There on a straight-back wooden chair sat an older bedraggled man. A short stool sat in front of him, and it held a jelly glass filled with bright yellow pencils. A small sign advertised them at a quarter a piece. Daddy knelt beside him, took out his wallet, removed some bills, and placed them in one of the man's hands. When he offered some pencils in return, Daddy declined. "We have plenty of pencils at home, but thank you anyway."

I had moved to the center of the vestibule when Daddy walked over to me. I felt his hand on my shoulder once again as he spoke these words: "Verily I say unto you, Inasmuch as ye have done it unto one of the least of these my brethren, ye have done it unto me."

Then he draped his arm around my shoulder and said gently: "Come on, Ran, we have to buy a squirter."

Ray

Ray Clark Farris loved snow. He cherished every flake he ever saw fall, every snowball he ever threw, and every snowman we ever built. And when the snows came, Ray would be the first to our door, gloved and rubber-booted, his green parka zipped to the chin, its fur-trimmed hood close about his face, unable to contain his impatience with anyone not already outside. "Hurry," he would say, "it won't last long."

Just an inch or two closed the school, and it even cancelled church if it came on Sunday or Wednesday. There was a double treat for a boy. The snow lay siege to our town, stopped what little traffic we had, and transformed the road in front of our house into a playground. No one we knew owned a sled, so we skated on the snow—ran and locked our knees and slid on the icy pavement. Sometimes we found a box at Mr. Green's store, flattened it, held on to the flaps, and skidded our way down the hill, almost to the gin.

Two or three times a day, we scooped up the softest snow, added sugar, milk, and vanilla flavoring, and whipped it into snow cream. Ray insisted we eat it outside to keep it from melting. "Let's mix up another batch, freeze it, and eat it on the Fourth of July," he said once. "That way we can pretend."

Even then, Ray and I had an unspoken understanding. We were ten-year-old romantics, and both of us loved the beauty the snow dealt our town, loved its power to conceal and transform. Only now do I recognize the shabbiness that surrounded my youth: the tar-papered store across the street, the rusted gin and seed house, the hog houses and the Mule Barn, all ramshackle and pathetic. But when the snow came, it swirled everything together and rendered it holy and sublime. The snow allowed us, if only for a while, to live in an enchanted place where time was frozen with the elements and all was right with the world.

Finally, the sun came back from beyond the Equator and vanquished the cold, drew it from the streams, and the land, and the attics of houses, forced it into the open where the March winds could blow it away. Only the slyest remnants remained, hidden deep in the dark of fruit cellars, caves, and in the bottoms of wells. The cycle began again, and if Ray and I were fortunate, in a few months the snow would take us once again to that magical world that only boys can know.

Mama and the Murdered
Telephone Operator

Many who read these words about a real telephone will be confused. To you, it is a computer that serves as an encyclopedia, a dictionary, a grammar book, a foreign language translator, a biblical concordance, a camera, a map, a woman's voice that directs you on your automobile trip, and a guide to all manner of biographies and machinery. It is a poetry anthology and an art gallery. A real telephone is none of those things. It is a device that allows people to speak with one another.

Why anyone refers to this unfortunate modern gadget as a telephone is a mystery to me. One thing it does well is help people be rude. I rarely go out to eat anymore because so many other diners talk out loud on their devices, and I can't tolerate such ill-mannered behavior. Neither can I abide two adults seated together punching their keyboards without regarding their table companions. Such a lack of manners makes me want to ask this question: "If you are so tired of each other, why do you waste your time in each other's company?"

We were slow getting a telephone. Our entire

family and I were thrilled that summer day in 1958 when the man installed ours on the sewing machine in the dining room. It was a wooden box with a crank and a Bakelite mouthpiece and separate earpiece, one for each hand. This occurred after Mama worked as an operator for the telephone company, so she knew a lot about our new gadget. She also understood what everyone referred to as the "party line."

Don't let this confuse you. I don't mean the kind of party that people have on their birthdays. We and two other households used the same telephone line. We knew to answer our phone only when it rang two times. Two other families answered on one or three rings. Of course, we could pick up the receiver and eavesdrop on both of the other lines, just as they could listen to us. It was common for all three homes to hear and announce: "I know you're on the line listening. Please hang up."

Years later, we got a black dial phone with a seven-digit number. It allowed us to make our own local calls, but if it went outside of our area, we had to go through the long-distance operator. Her office was in Lawrenceburg, around fifteen or twenty miles north of our town of St. Joseph.

One night late, Daddy was working the graveyard shift, my sister Vicki was out on a date, and my sister Deanna had married, moved to Alabama, and had a child. "Let's call Deedy and see how the baby is doing," Mama said about nine o'clock. We went to the sewing machine, and Mother dialed "0" for the central telephone office in Lawrenceburg. No answer. "Well," Mother said, as she clicked off the phone and dialed again. This time it rang constantly for over a minute, and then she hung up.

Then I tried and counted twenty-five unanswered rings. Nothing. Mama starting jerking open the drawers of the sewing machine cabinet. "What are you doing, Mama?" I said, sure she was about to explode.

"Looking for this." She ripped through the pages of the phone book and found the number for the Lawrence County Sheriff's Office. She tore at the dial.

"Mama," I said, but caught myself and hushed.

"Hello? Is this Sheriff Davis? Well, I want to talk to him. I don't care if he is upstairs asleep. I voted for him, and I mean to speak to him right now. You go up there and tell him that Marie Cross from St. Joe is on the phone."

Two minutes passed. "Sheriff Davis, this is Marie Cross in St. Joe, and I'd like to report a murder. Yes, sir, a murder. I don't know, but if you go up to the telephone office there in Lawrenceburg, you'll find the operator dead on the floor in a pool of blood." She hung up.

"Mama."

"Hush," she said.

I hushed and waited for prison.

Fifteen minutes later, the operator called, open for business.

"Is this Mrs. Cross?"

"Yes, it is," Mama said, like she might have been talking to the preacher.

"The sheriff and a deputy just came by here and said you told them I had been murdered. What were you doing? What do you think—"

"You hush," Mama said. "I've been trying to get you for thirty minutes. When you didn't answer, I thought somebody had killed you. If somebody had, you'd be glad I called."

"I've been busy," the operator said.

"Don't start with that," Mama said. "You've probably been with friends drinking coffee in the break room or with some of your buddies on the phone. And one more thing: from now on I'm giving you three rings, three rings mind you, and you won't ever know when it's me. If you don't answer by then, I'm calling the sheriff every time. Now you hush and put through this call."

"Hey, Deedy," Mama said in her sweet voice. "How's the baby?"

After we finished talking, the phone rang. "Mrs. Cross? This is Sheriff Davis. I want to thank you for calling and to let you know that the operator is fine. If you ever need me again, you call any time."

Sheriff Davis went undefeated as long as he ran for office. Elections are good things, aren't they?

We never had trouble reaching that operator again.

Dancing

We didn't go on vacation when I was a boy, or anywhere else. Except church. Boy did we go to church. I mean we went to church all the time. You couldn't go to church more than we went to church. It would have been physically impossible. The Apostle Paul did not go to church more than we went to church. Sunday morning, Sunday night, Wednesday night, Vacation Bible School, Tent Meetings, Singings, Revivals, Bible Bowls, Gospel Meetings, and Dinner on the Ground. And if my parents had found a way to enroll me in Women's Bible Study on Tuesday mornings, they would have done that, too. I mean we were instant in season and out, reproving, rebuking, and exhorting one another in Psalms, hymns, and spiritual songs. Go ye therefore and do likewise.

The church we attended was against a lot more than it was for, especially those things that make you feel good all over more than anywhere else. You know, stuff like smoking, chewing, and public bathing. All on the same page.

But at the very top of that forbidden list, however, was dancing—or "dainsing" as we called it. Our church could not tolerate dancing. And yet with a strange inconsistency, two or three times a year, they loaded us all up on the Joy Bus: JOY. Jesus, Others, Yourself. Then they drove us down to Florence to the North Alabama Skating Rink. There all us boys and girls strapped on our skates, held hands, and started gliding around that rink to the same music they played down at the honky-tonk. Sometimes people tripped and fell, boys and girls in there together. I liked falling.

We had a good time at the rink because we were dancing, with wheels on our feet, which kept everything right. All you young people be admonished.

My First Semester in College

During my first semester in college, an English professor called me aside. "Mr. Cross," he said, "after hearing you speak and reading your essays, it is apparent that you are one of our more provincial students." I thanked him and basked for hours in the light of his opinion of me. And then I looked up that word, provincial: "uncultured, unrefined, a person from the country lacking urban sophistication and broad mindedness." Following a great deal of reflection and deflation, I realized that his aim was accurate. He had hit the bull's eye dead center, and I had trouble sweeping up any remnants of a compliment. I was, after all, from St. Joseph, Tennessee, and knew little of the ways of the outside world.

Oh, I knew how to harness and plow a mule, kill hogs, make sausage, and render out lard, but I would not have known foie gras from a goose's liver. No, I have not always been the intellectual Gibraltar whose words you are reading right now. The fact that I never amounted to anything cannot be blamed on my boyhood. After all, I was brought up surrounded by institutions of higher education: Johnny Odem's mill, Wes Cross's store, Raleigh Green's store, Tom

McKinney's gin, and Lon Odem's Mule Barn. The scholars in our town gathered at those noble venues most every day to visit, talk, laugh, tell stories, and contemplate the problems of the human heart. I'm going to be telling you some stories about those men as we go along.

But let me tell you about one thing as a teacher that perturbs me. It's when I have students who feel intellectually deficient because they come from small towns. What an unfortunate attitude that is.

History suggests that the opposite is more accurate. Mark Twain was born in Florida, Missouri, a town of one hundred people. Shakespeare came from Stratford, a tiny hamlet in England. If you've been there, you know.

But let's bring this a little closer to our Alabama home. Helen Keller was from Tuscumbia; W.C. Handy from Florence; Jesse Owens was from Oakville; Percy Sledge from Leighton; Mr. Sonny James himself was from Hackleburg.

The names of these Alabama towns, barely pinpoints on a map of the world. The names of the people, exclamation points that touch the sky.

The Army

Ijoined the Tennessee Army National Guard in February of 1970 and left for Army Basic Training at Fort Jackson, South Carolina, a few weeks later. I was nineteen years old. I recall everything about that day because I was scared; I had arrived in a strange universe. All of the old veterans I knew back at home gave me the same advice: "Don't volunteer for nothing. Do your best to keep the sergeants from knowing your name. You just want to be third man, third squad. Nothing and nobody else. No additional identifiers. If the sergeants call a soldier's name, he's in trouble. They never use it to brag on him. Only to humiliate him and belittle him in front of his comrades."

A friend of mine picked me up at home early that morning to take me to the bus station which would lead me to the Nashville Airport. He, my father, and I walked out together. When we reached the car, I noticed that Mother wasn't with us. I ran back into the house and found her leaning on the kitchen cabinet shaking and crying. I decided immediately that lying to her would be the proper thing to do. "Don't cry, Mama. I've wanted to go to the Army for a long time and always looked forward to this day." I bent down, took her in my arms, and kissed her face, trying in vain to conceal my lie.

I went back outside alone. Just before I got into the car, Daddy walked over close beside me. He had been drafted into the Army at the outbreak of World War Two. I knew he'd have some final words to say to me before I left. He reached up in the gentle way he had and draped his arm over my shoulder. He squeezed me and patted my back. "Well, Ran," he said. "They'll pay you, and they'll feed you."

As my friend and I started backing out of the driveway, Daddy came to attention and rendered us the hand salute and held it until we were out of sight. I can still see the pride in his eyes.

Late that afternoon, our plane landed at the Columbia, South Carolina, airport. An olive drab bus was waiting for us. A drill instructor was there to drive us to the post. Our first stop was a red brick building. When the bus stopped, the DI began to yell at us to get off and form two lines leading inside. "Enter the building and stand at attention with your back against the wall. Be prepared to do whatever you are told to do."

I had never seen needles so huge as those the medics wielded.

Once the vials were filled with our blood, the DI marched us next door to the mess hall. "Everybody!"

the Drill Instructor screamed. "Get in line, get your food, eat up, and get out." Then he jumped atop a table in the middle of the mess hall and began to scream: "Eat up and get out. Eat up and get out." Over and over.

The truth in Daddy's words began to resonate: "They'll feed you."

All of us new soldiers were still wearing the civilian clothes we had arrived in. The DI marched us to the supply room, and the sergeant in charge issued us pillows, sheets, and blankets. When we reached the barracks that would be home for a while, all of us were ready to collapse in our bunks. A few days later, we marched to a huge warehouse where we were issued uniforms, hats, shoes, boots, socks, and military underwear. A long line formed at a sewing machine that produced name tapes sewn above the right shirt pocket. Mine, of course, said CROSS.

That day after lunch, we had our first formation in uniform. I think we all felt like soldiers for the first time. "Now listen up," the DI said. "We're about to have our first police call. Who knows what that is?" Not a hand went up, and no one spoke. "It's not what it sounds like," the sergeant said. "It means we're going to scour this entire area for trash, and nothing will be left that doesn't belong. I have a question that will get us started. How many stinking college boys do we have here?" No one spoke, and no one raised a hand. I had been to college, but I certainly was not going to volunteer. "Do you see that white building?" the DI asked. "That's the orderly room, and it contains all of your records. I'm going to go inside and read every word on file. I'll find out who my stinking college boys are. All of you who have lied to me will be awfully sorry."

I raised my hand, and so did a boy in the last squad. "Post!" the DI yelled. "That means get up here by me on the double. You're already late right now." The other stinking college student and I tore out running as ordered and stood facing the sergeant at attention. "Here's what I want you to do. Exactly this way with no exceptions. Get down on your stomachs and low crawl across this entire area picking up anything that doesn't belong. Listen to what I'm about to say: If it ain't green, it don't grow, it don't wiggle, or God didn't make it, pick it up."

After several minutes, the DI hollered "Post" for us once again. We stood in front of him with cupped hands. "Present contraband," he said. We held a variety of trash: pop tops, cigarette butts, candy wrappers, and various other items one might find on such a mission.

Then it happened. As the sergeant was gazing into my hands, I saw him reach and withdraw one half of a dead oak leaf which he waved in my face. Then he stared at the name on my uniform: Cross. "Cross is a mighty strange name for an atheist. You are an atheist, aren't you, Cross?"

"No, Drill Sergeant."

"Who made this leaf?" he said.

"God made it, Drill Sergeant."

"Remember what I told you. If it ain't green, it don't grow, it don't wiggle, or God didn't make it, pick it up. Right now drop into the front leaning rest position and give me ten push-ups for disobeying a direct order. Remember: If you ain't counting, I'm not."

I started. "One Drill Sergeant, two Drill Sergeant, three Drill Sergeant"—all the way to ten.

"Now," he said, "drop and give God ten push-ups for denying His glory. Remember: If you ain't counting, He's not."

I started. "One God, two God, three God"—all the way to ten.

I spent thirty-one and a half years in the military, but I never spent a more extraordinary time than the day I was required to give God ten push-ups for picking up a leaf He had made.

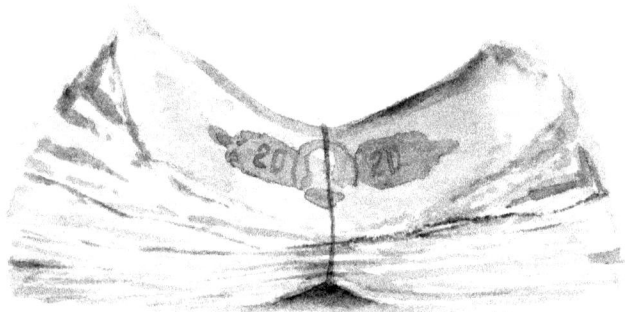

Change Money?

When I was ten, my family and I went to Water Valley, Mississippi, to visit my mother's Aunt Ide. It was the only vacation we ever took, but somewhere on those curving, tar-and-gravel roads, wanderlust seized my soul, and during the next two decades, I laid for a chance to travel again. After graduate school when I was offered a job in Brazil, I knew the time had come. And despite the magnificence of Water Valley—with its paved streets and watermelon festival, it had not prepared me for life in Rio de Janeiro, The Marvelous City.

As soon as the plane landed, I realized how helpless I had suddenly become. Have you heard the lie that English will take you all over the world? When I stepped off the plane in Rio, I instantly became deaf, mute, and illiterate. All the announcements at the airport were in Portuguese, as well as all the signs. If I recall, even the arrows pointed in Portuguese. I just walked around—trying to look pitiful and succeeding—offering my passport to anyone in a uniform.

Finally, two airport security officers took me into custody and began interrogating me—in Portuguese—

to no avail, although I kept repeating, "Me no speaky Portuguese." Once they realized I was not going to answer their questions, they summoned a man in a suit who, after thumbing through my passport several times, finally said this to me: "Why are you in Brazil?"

I just knew they were going to put dope in my suitcase and lock me up for the rest of my life in a Brazilian prison with water dripping from the ceiling. It was time to act, to jerk the big lanyard. Or, as they taught us when I was a soldier in Officer Candidate School: "In a crisis, do something, even if it's wrong." My military training kicked in. I came to attention and said in my finest command voice: "I was sent here by the Congress of the United States of America to teach English at the University of Rio de Janeiro as a Fulbright Scholar." That worked. The man in the suit extended his hand, smiled, and said: "Sir, welcome to Brazil."

Once I collected my luggage, I still had no idea of where to go. Finally, I saw a line of people at what appeared to be the customs station, so I joined that group. Once the agent went through my bags, he stamped my passport and pointed toward an exit. As I walked through the electric sliding door, I realized that I was about to be outside. I was still confused, but only for a moment.

There, standing on the sidewalk was a woman

holding a sign with two words painted in huge black letters: Randy Cross. Directly behind her parked by the curb was a huge car with an American Consulate flag attached to the fender. A gentleman in a suit sat behind the steering wheel. Still a few feet away, I said in a loud voice: "I am Randy Cross."

The woman lowered the sign, put out her hand, smiled, and said, "Professor Cross, welcome to Rio de Janeiro."

I wanted to hug her neck, but we shook hands instead. Many years have passed since that day, but whenever anyone asks me the best thing I have ever read, I answer immediately with the truth: Randy Cross.

On our drive into the city, she gave me a lot of useful information pertaining to the university where I would be teaching, what to expect from the students, and the role the American Consulate would play in my life during the coming months. She talked about Rio's economy and where and with whom I should trade my U.S. dollars for Brazilian cruzeiros. I learned a great deal about a money changer named Lucas, mainly that a bank would give me one hundred and forty cruzeiros per dollar while Lucas would give me two hundred and eighty. She gave me his address, directions to his apartment, and told me how many times I should knock on his door.

We rode for nearly an hour through various sections of the Marvelous City before we arrived at the Hotel Debret where the Consulate had booked me for one week. I was tired from my journey and ready to relax.

What an extraordinary place I found myself in. The day before when I flew out of the Huntsville, Alabama, airport on that February morning, the temperature was twenty-seven degrees. When we left the plane onto the tarmac in Rio the next day, it was one hundred and five. I can still easily recall the wave of heat that slammed into my face when I stepped onto the platform at the top of the stairs. At first, I thought it was heat from the 747 engines that engulfed us, but I was wrong. It was merely the sun shining down from the South American sky on a typical summer day. I knew but had forgotten that the seasons at the top and bottom of the world exchange places.

Aside from these services the Consulate provided, they arranged for a rental agent to drive me around the city and help me find an apartment. She was a lovely woman who spoke perfect English. On one drive through the city, she asked me if I saw anything that appealed to me. I told her that I was not interested in the appearance, I just wanted some place safe. She reached over, patted my arm, and said, "Oh, my dear, there are no safe places in Rio. Just let me know when something looks good to you."

A few minutes later, we approached an apartment building in the suburb of Leme (Lemmy), one block from the most famous beach on earth, Copacabana. I rented a wonderful apartment there at 710 Rua Gustavo Sampaio (setchy sintose e daish Hoo uh Gooshtahvo Sam pie oh.)

The following morning, I set off on what I believed to be my most exciting adventure of all, dying at the hands of a black marketeer. I located the building, rode the elevator up to the seventh floor, found the door, and knocked four times as instructed. "Lucas," I whispered.

After the sound of sliding dead bolts, the door opened, revealing the back of a man walking away from me down the hall. I didn't want to, but I followed.

When I entered the room, he was seated behind a desk. In stacks at least a foot high, blue, green, red, and brown cruzeiro notes rose up like miniature skyscrapers, covering the desktop. In the middle of the stacks lay a .44 Magnum, its eight-inch barrel pointed at my stomach. He did not speak.

I lifted my hands slowly in front of me like I might have been warming them at a fire, eased two fingers into a front pants pocket, extracted my five one-hundred-dollar bills, and placed them carefully, individually, between the pistol and a tower of blue money. The five pictures of Benjamin Franklin stared back up at me. I still remember feeling as though I had betrayed him. Lucas scooped up the dollars like a hand of poker, examined them carefully, and placed them in a drawer. As he punched the numbers on his adding machine, it rattled out the printed results: one million, forty thousand cruzeiros. It was a noble enough looking sum to me, so I nodded, and he began demolishing his colorful buildings in banded twenty-bill packs. Without counting, I began stuffing them in all four pockets, like a congressman in the Abscam scandal. When I ran out of pockets, I began stuffing money wherever I could: socks, armpits, and the waistband of my pants. I transformed my entire body into a walking bank vault.

As a Southerner, I wanted to thank him, to tell him I was pleased to meet him, that I thought Rio was lovely—something. But I could do nothing but turn—slowly—and walk from the room a millionaire, both ears focused on the hammer of the forty-four.

During the coming months, I learned that "Lucas" was only a code word, not anyone's name. Later, when I had learned enough Portuguese, I merely made a phone call, and a Lucas courier would deliver cruzeiros to my house. I even began writing him checks on my Decatur, Alabama, bank; he cashed them without question. Once, I told a friend that at home, out-of-town and out-of-state checks were almost impossible to cash, let alone out-of-hemisphere ones. "Nobody writes bad checks to Lucas," he said.

I know I never did.

The longer I lived in Rio, the more I came to know about the currency market below the Equator. All over the city, men stood in shops or on street corners rubbing together their index finger tips with their thumbs, the international symbol for money. Once we got near to each other, he would whisper "Change money?" I learned to respond, "Nao, obrigado." ("No, thank you.") I was, after all, a loyal customer of Lucas since the day I became a millionaire in his office.

Fred, who is still one of my favorite people on earth, was a student in my American Culture class at the University of Rio de Janeiro when I was a Fulbright Scholar there. I owe a great deal of gratitude to Senator J. William Fulbright from Arkansas for providing me the honor of living and teaching in Brazil and Portugal.

On the first day of the term, I took a U. S. map to class so I could show the students where I had lived in Tennessee, Alabama, and Mississippi. I wanted them to be able to picture the places I mentioned in the stories I told. When the class ended, several students remained behind to meet me and make me feel welcome. I knew I had come to a fine place. I felt as though I was back at home in the South.

Of all the students, Fred was the last to leave. "I saw that you lived in Tennessee," he said. "Do you like Elvis?" I told him I loved Elvis and was sorry he was gone. Then Fred asked me to show him the location where I grew up so he could see how close my hometown of St. Joseph was to Memphis. "Have you seen Graceland?" he asked. When I said "yes," he moaned out loud. Then he said, "Have you seen Elvis's statue on Beale Street?" I said I had, and he made another deep sound from his throat, wrapped his arms around each other and rubbed them as his eyes turned red. I knew right then that we were going to be buddies, and I was right. We both played guitar, and Fred even taught me to make some of the chords that grace the songs of Brazilian songwriter Tom Jobim.

I had a great time in the American Culture class. I didn't know I would be teaching it until our first faculty meeting a few days before the term began. "Where is the textbook?" I asked the department chair, a refined, courteous, and intelligent gentleman.

"We don't have any textbooks," he said. "Just talk to the students about whatever you please. All they know about the United States is John Wayne and McDonald's." The professor had a fine sense of humor as the textbook episode displays.

Nevertheless, I took his advice and talked about my favorite segments of American culture. I began with the arrival of the *Mayflower* in 1620. After several class meetings where we discussed the Puritans and the Indians, I was ready for us to move on to the eighteenth century.

Our classroom was huge and swallowed up the twenty-five or so students—all English majors—who met there twice each week. The floor was made of polished concrete that glowed from the overhead lights. In the left corner at the rear of the room, a few metal chairs waited for any visitors who might like to join us. On the first day of our new topic, I began class with this statement: "Please raise your hand if you know who Thomas Jefferson was." I expected at least half of the students to do so, but not one did. They just sat there silent, not moving, not even looking around. I didn't know how to respond.

Then, the most memorable time I ever had in a class took place. Without uttering a sound, Fred stood and walked to the rear of the classroom and took hold of the back of one of the guest chairs. As he dragged it across the concrete floor, the sound was similar to a set of squealing, worn-out, automobile brakes. He dragged it slowly toward the front of the room where I stood, confused, behind my lectern. The students remained quiet and still.

When Fred arrived, he placed the chair a couple of feet from me. "Please sit here," he said, pointing to the chair. I sat down, and he stepped behind the lectern and raised his hands like the conductor of an orchestra. "Please quote along with me," he said. "We'll start on three. One, two, three." The entire class began at exactly the same time and finished that way.

"We hold these truths to be self-evident, that all men are created equal, that they are endowed by their Creator with certain unalienable Rights, that among these are Life, Liberty, and the pursuit of Happiness."

I began to weep at the same time the class started to recite Jefferson's words. When the students completed their final syllable, my face was red and wet with tears. "I am so ashamed that I treated all of you so shabbily. I suspect that most classes in America could not quote that entire passage from the Declaration of Independence. I apologize for doubting your knowledge."

Fred walked over to the chair where I remained seated and patted me on the back. "It's all right," he said. "For you and your fellow citizens, the Declaration of Independence is a truth. For us Brazilians, it remains only a dream."

I realized then that I was getting more from my students than they would ever learn from me. They inhabited one of the most magnificent places on earth, from the ocean, the beaches, the mountains, and the sky that held the glowing sun each day and the Southern Cross at night. Lucas changed my money, but those extraordinary people changed my life.

God bless you, Senator Fulbright.

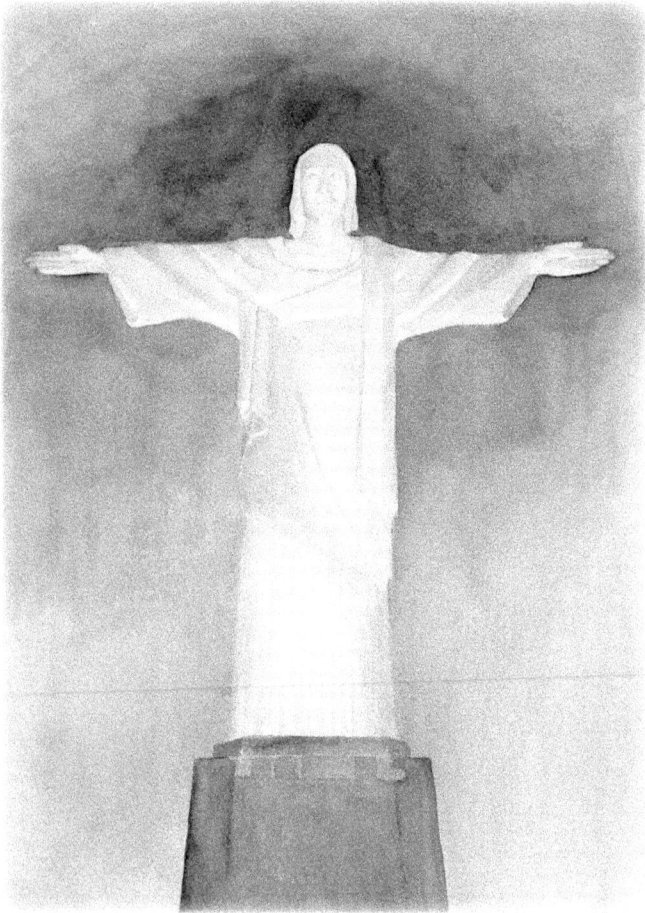

The Murdered Man in Rio

Several years ago, I experienced a time of wonder in my life I could never repeat. I had the privilege of serving for one year as a Fulbright Professor of English at the University of Rio de Janeiro. Having grown up in St. Joseph, Tennessee, a town of five hundred people, Rio's population of almost ten million kept me in awe during my entire stay in Brazil. Aside from the beautiful mountains—including Sugar Loaf and Corcovado—and the lovely architecture, I lived just off one of the most breathtaking paradises on earth, Copacabana Beach, which merged into Ipanema. I could never walk there without smiling as my mind recalled the words and melody of Tom Jobim: "Tall and tan and young and lovely, the Girl From Ipanema goes walking. And when she passes, each one she passes goes 'ah.'"

My favorite time there occurred when my parents came and stayed with me for several weeks. The most memorable thing about my apartment on the 25th floor was the views out my windows. From the front, I could see the grandeur of Sugar Loaf Mountain, but the amazing scene was out my rear window: the statue of Christ the Redeemer which stood atop Corcovado

Mountain. It was extraordinary at all hours but especially at night when the spotlights illuminated the statue and caused the Christ to appear suspended between Heaven and Earth.

When my parents came to visit, I made sure that the curtains were closed on their day of arrival. Only after complete darkness engulfed the city did I call them to the rear window. "Stand facing the curtains," I said. When they were in position, I flung open the drapes.

My parents moaned at the sight of the illuminated Christ standing in the black sky. "Law," Mama said. "That's the biggest Jesus I've ever seen." Within a few days, my Brazilian friends, my parents, and I always referred to Christ the Redeemer as The Big Jesus. After all these years, that glorious image emerges from my memory, and I'm standing at that rear window with my dear parents.

A few days later, we were out for a stroll on Copacabana where Sugar Loaf stood at the far end of the beach. "My goodness," Mama said. "I remember seeing a picture of Sugar Loaf Mountain in our geography book when I was in the seventh grade. I never dreamed I would ever see it in person. Thank you, son, for making this possible."

"Oh, Mama, I'm the one who should do the thanking. If not for the support and encouragement from you and Daddy, I could never have been here. You sent me to college, paid my rent, bought me cars and clothes, and constantly displayed your faith in my abilities. I would never have been here without you." What a lucky boy I was.

One afternoon the three of us were strolling along the sidewalk in Ipanema when it began to rain. We were about two miles from my apartment and attempted to hail a cab. No luck. As in all big cities, the taxis fill up as soon as the rain begins to pour. I knew better than to put us on a city bus, but I didn't want my parents to get soaked, especially if we had to walk for miles in that storm. I guided us to the nearest bus stop where we got in line with at least a dozen others seeking refuge.

When the bus finally arrived, all the seats were filled, and other passengers stood crowded in the aisle. We joined them. People standing were pushing, shuffling, stepping on toes, coughing, talking loudly, rocking back and forth, and placing their hands on other passengers' shoulders and backs. At last we arrived at the bus stop nearest my apartment, and the three of us squirmed our way through what was left of the soaking, dissatisfied sojourners. As we entered the shelter, Daddy said, "Something is wrong. All of my money is gone. Somebody must have got it on the bus. I remember a man who kept putting his hands on me."

"He was probably a decoy," I said, "someone to occupy your mind while the thief stole your money. That sort of thing happens often on Rio buses. Everybody picks everybody else's pockets. If you stay on long enough, you can get your own wallet back."

And then it struck: Hurricane Marie. When Mama got mad, there was no apologizing her back to normal. Her anger had to run its course, and woe be to anyone who attempted to placate her. After fussing at Daddy for getting robbed, she took a turn at the thief and everyone who knew him. Next came the bus driver for letting such trash be one of his passengers. "He had to know who that stinking thief was, and he still let him on." Then she took on the Rio Police Department and the Mayor. Daddy and I knew enough to allow her category five winds to continue to blow. Interference in her diatribe at this point would have intensified the storm, so we allowed her to rave on. It was the safest thing to do.

Two weeks passed. One morning around this time, we decided to walk down to Copacabana. As we left the apartment that morning, Elias, our fine and dignified porter, smiled, nodded his head, and greeted us in his usual manner: "Bon dia." (That's "good day" in English but pronounced "bone-zhee-uh" in Portuguese.). As we left the building, Elias spoke and motioned with his index finger for me to come close to him. In a whisper, he asked if we were going for a walk. If so, he said that we should not take our usual route down the sidewalk past the bakery. We should go in the opposite direction instead. "Some horrible thing has occurred that you do not want your parents to see."

When I turned around, Mother was leaning toward Elias and me, trying to hear what we were talking about. "What was he saying to you?" Mama asked me.

"He said that a new gift store had opened up in the opposite direction we were headed and that you might find some things there you'd like to take to friends back home."

"He didn't do it. People don't whisper about shopping. I asked you what he was talking about, and I want you to tell me what it was right now."

"He said something bad had happened down the sidewalk in front of the bakery. You and Daddy stay here with Elias, and I'll run down there and see what's happening. I'll hurry straight back up here and let you know what's going on."

When I reached the block near the bakery, I could see the crowd that had gathered. I made my way through. There lying on his back was the first—and I hope the last—murdered man I had ever seen. Three bullet holes pierced his face and forehead. His eyes were locked open, staring at the blue Brazilian sky. I quickly made up a lie to take with me back up the sidewalk: "An elderly woman has fallen and sprained her ankle, and they are going to get her up and take her home. Everything is going to be fine."

When I turned around to go back and deliver my good news, I ran smack into Mother. She had followed me down to the bakery without me knowing it. As gently as possible, I reached over and took her hand. "Come on, Mama," I said softly, "let's go."

She jerked her hand out of mine, pointed down at the lifeless man at our feet, and said for all to hear: "I hope that's the man who robbed your daddy."

"Mama," I said, "that's not the man who robbed Daddy. That was far from here on the other side of town. That's probably a drug dealer."

"Good," Mama said. "He needed killing. Go get your daddy so he can see."

I did what she said and brought Daddy down to see the spectacle. We stood there for less than a minute when Mama said, "Come on, let's go for a walk." The three of us took hands as she said, "Isn't that music pretty coming down from the hills? Let's ease on down to the beach and find us some ice cream. Wouldn't that be good on such a hot day? Thanks again for bringing us to this beautiful city, Randy Boy. I don't think we'll ever be the same."

And she was right.

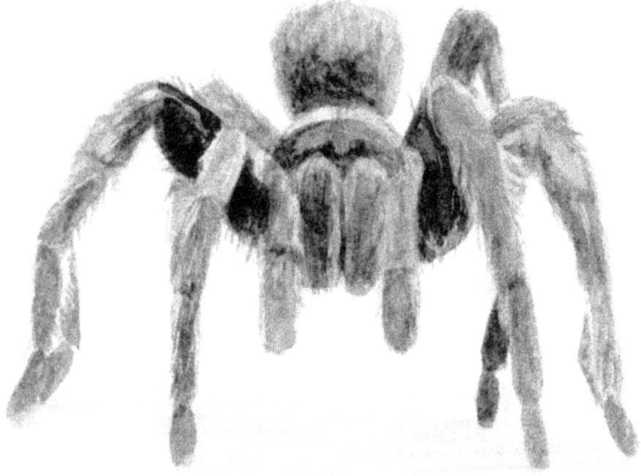

The Amazon

Of all the adventures I have encountered, none has been so thrilling as the one I shared with my cousin Don in the Amazon Jungle. At the time, I was living in Brazil and teaching at the University of Rio de Janeiro. One evening Don and I were talking on the phone, and we made plans for him to come to Rio in a couple of weeks. During that conversation, he asked if we could visit the Amazon. I told him I would make the arrangements to coincide with his visit, and I went to a travel agency the next day. The person there booked flights to and from Manaus, a huge and beautiful city in the northern Amazon. He also arranged for a guide named Carlos to meet us at the hotel on the day we arrived.

When the guide got there, he took us down to a pier where a river boat was docked. After we boarded, we could see the large number of passengers. Once we left the shore, we cruised down the magnificent Amazon River for about an hour before the pilot docked. Here Carlos, Don, and I left the boat and went ashore. Some of the crew brought a flat bottom motorboat to the shore. Then the river boat continued its voyage leaving the three of us alone on the edge of the beautiful world we had just discovered.

We loaded our provisions in the boat, and Carlos steered us along the shore of backwater which flowed through a huge grove of trees. The river's main body eased by. Attempting to see the opposite bank was like trying to detect the other side of an ocean. After several minutes of motoring through the swampy jungle, we arrived at a straw hut situated on an elevated piece of land. We docked and carried our belongings inside. It was a neat building that contained two lanterns hanging from the ceiling and three hammocks spaced neatly around the room. Each was covered with a mosquito net that hung from the top of the hammock frame and was tightly wrapped around the bunk all the way to the floor. Its job was to eliminate the threat of the creatures that flew and crawled throughout the jungle night.

Once we were settled in, Carlos prepared our supper with food he brought from Manaus. Just after we finished eating and the sun began to dim, a native man wearing a loin cloth arrived in a dugout with a push pole in one hand and a spear in the other. He stood at the bow of the boat.

"Who is that?" I asked Carlos.

"He is a caiman hunter," he said. "Some say alligator and not caiman. He will take us hunting." With Carlos's interesting language skills, my dab of Portuguese, and Cousin Don's Tennessee English, we kept a linguistic holiday going all the time.

I looked at Don when the issue of alligator

hunting arose. I could tell from his eyes that he voted no, just as I did.

"We don't want to hunt alligators," I said.

Carlos responded with "I promised to pay when we returned. We must go now, or he will be upset. You don't want to see that." We lit the lanterns and set out for our adventure.

The setting sun and the shadows cast by the rainforest produced an eerie atmosphere. We climbed into the dugout behind the hunter who remained standing at the front with his spear raised above his shoulder. Don eased down in the middle on the right, I took the left, and Carlos sat in the rear with a huge multi-cell flashlight. Once we were halfway between the hut and the edge of the forest, Carlos gave us a warning. "If we turn over or fall out of the boat, swim to that shore," he said, pointing to the hut. "Don't swim to the close bank there to our left. That's where the alligators build their nests. They will catch you, pull you down, trap you, and eat you during the days to come."

"Well, Cousin Don, that lets me know that I only need to swim faster than you, not the alligators." I said those words to a man who had been a lifeguard for years. He smiled and thanked me for the advice although he knew he could swim faster than I could with an anvil chained around his neck.

At about this time, Carlos turned on his flashlight and dragged the beam of light across the dark water.

As it moved to left and right and back, it revealed at least twenty glowing red embers floating on the surface of the water. Don and I attempted in vain to decipher the mystery, and then Carlos placed the flashlight in his lap and clapped his hands together. As he shined the light back to the same location, we watched the glowing red circles disappear several feet from the dugout. We all sat silent until the waves from the submerging alligators reached the bow of our boat. The hunter poled us to the spot where we had seen the glowing eyes, raised his spear, and thrust it into the black water and through the neck of a small alligator which he placed beside his feet near the bow. Only seconds passed before Don hollered and leapt to his feet. "Something just rammed me in the side," he said. The boat rocked violently, and water poured in on both sides. Carlos demanded loudly that Don sit back down before we sank.

"Don't raise your voice to me," Don said. "I didn't grow up in your world. Every splashing sound I hear is a ten-foot alligator attempting to eat us."

Then the problem manifested itself. On the bottom of the boat a white fish was twisting and flopping on the floor. The two Amazonians determined that it was attracted to the flashlight and flew through the air to tackle it.

Just as the commotion ceased, the hunter speared another alligator and placed it beside the first one. Carlos asked him to turn the boat around and take us back to the shore near the hut. He could tell that Don and I had experienced enough adventure for one night.

When the hunter unloaded us, we eased down and stretched out on the peaceful shore. I was taken with the soft glow of the hut in the black jungle and decided to climb into my hammock and rest up for the next day. Don and Carlos remained by the moonlit river laughing and talking about the day's adventures. I eased up one corner of the mosquito net and slid into the hammock on my back.

I lay there for a few minutes while I grew accustomed to the soft glow of the lanterns. At one point, my eyes were drawn to a drooping fold of the net that hung a few inches above my head. There near my face hung the largest tarantula spider I had ever seen. I froze with fear. I could hear my companions talking and laughing, but I could not figure out a safe way to get their attention. I cleared my throat, faked a cough, and tried to whistle without drawing the tarantula's attention. He remained upside down dangling from the inside of the net. Once I decided I had no choice, I raised my voice and said "Don." Then much louder, "Don!" The spider remained still.

I held my breath and heard Don say aloud: "Carlos, that's my cousin's voice. He sounds like something is wrong. Let's go see what's going on." They showed up a minute later without speaking. When they arrived, I didn't speak, and I didn't move a finger. Carlos did both.

"It is a tair-en-toola. Do not disturb heem. If you do, he will fall on your face and make many bites."

I took Carlos's advice and didn't move at all. Without speaking again or touching the net in any place, they returned to the little beach we had used earlier.

A few minutes later, Don spoke to me from there in a loud whisper: "Remember, Randy. Do not disturb heem."

This was the worst predicament I had ever faced. I could lie there beneath the dangerous spider and wait to be attacked or rely on nature to lead him back into the arms of the jungle. The second option caused me to close my eyes and wait for silence and sleep to banish the fear and the danger.

I do not recall my companions coming back to the hut and getting in their hammocks, but I do remember the tair-en-toola being gone the next morning.

Carlos told us to gather up our gear and we would go fishing while on our way back to Manaus. We pulled into the backwater in the boat and eased along for a few miles before arriving at a village on the grassless, hard-packed shore. Its dozen or so cabins sat on stilts at least ten or twelve feet tall. Several residents strolled about the buildings, and a group of tanned children swam just off the shore.

We brought out the fishing gear and began to cast into the dark water. As soon as hooks touched the surface, piranhas grabbed them. It was the first time I ever fished without bait. The smell on the hook from the previous catch enticed the next fish which we caught and released into the bottom of the boat. I can still see and hear the piranhas' sharp and pointed teeth gnawing on the hunting knife's bloody blade.

Later that afternoon, we loaded our equipment onto the river boat that took us back to Manaus where our extraordinary adventure began. It was here that we encountered the beautiful juxtaposition of the brown and black colors of the Amazon River. At Manaus they flow side by side for miles which is known as the Meeting of the Waters.

The next day, Don and I flew out of the beautiful city and looked down upon the most famous jungle in the world and the loveliest river on earth. Later that afternoon, we landed in Rio de Janeiro, home of Corcovado, Sugar Loaf Mountain, and the world's most famous beach, Copacabana.

What an extraordinary country Brazil is. I will never forget its kind people, the surreal scenery, and the night I slept in peace in the company of the tair-en-toola.

Tudo Bem

Fatima

Some years ago, my parents and I were strolling along a beautiful boulevard in Lisbon, Portugal. I was living there at the time serving as a Fulbright Scholar teaching American literature at the New University of Lisbon. As we walked along the sidewalk that day, we noticed two women on a bench speaking American English. When we were close enough to join their conversation, my father said, "I can understand what y'all are saying. Where are you from?"

"Michigan," one of them said.

"We're from Tennessee," my mother responded, using her quaint pronunciation of the state in a way I always loved.

"I thought you sounded Southern," the woman sneered.

My dear Mama, bless her heart, was in some ways like the Incredible Hulk. When something hit her the wrong way, there was no apologizing her back to normal. She would jolt to a stop with her face frozen in disgust. That's what happened then.

"How long have you been in Portugal?" the rude woman asked.

"We've been here two weeks," Mother said.

"So have you visited the Shrine of Fatima?"

"I don't know," Mama told her.

"Son," she said. "Have we been to that place?"

"No, ma'am," I said. "Not yet."

"You mean you've been here for two weeks, and you haven't visited the Shrine of Our Lady of Fatima? She was upset. Apparently, she was in that mood when we arrived.

"I don't even know who that is," Mother said.

"What do you mean you don't know who that is? We are talking about the Virgin Mary who became Our Lady of Fatima when she descended into a tree from Heaven in 1917 and prophesied to three farm children during several visits. She discussed the Bolshevik Revolution and predicted a second world war."

"Well, I don't believe that," Mother said. "You can believe what you want, and you can stand there and talk to me all day 'til you're blue in the face, but you ain't gonna get me to believe that Jesus's mama lit in no tree. She'd a been two thousand years old and looked just like a prune."

"Let's get out of here," she said to Daddy and me. And we did.

Rick and the Copperhead

I have never understood people who keep snakes for pets. Grown people. If you are one of them, please let me explain something to you that you have somehow missed. Snakes do not want to be petted. They want to bite you, strangle you, kill you if possible. Swallow your kittens headfirst.

A couple of years ago, my brother-in-law Rick Sims and I were walking in a creek bottom where we never should have been because snakes vacation there—when a three-foot copperhead ambushed him. It could have been me. After all these years, the fang marks are still visible on his right shin.

When the snake struck, Rick went directly to panic. He jumped straight up and commenced whooping and hollering and flailing around like a wind-sucking preacher on the Holy Ghost. He was squalling like a gut-shot house cat.

He had one of these little .410-guage shotgun pistols—ostensibly to protect us from those slithering devils—which he threw off into the bushes just as he began speaking in tongues and testifying. He sprang into the air over and over like a man on a trampoline.

When he landed the last time, he came down

with his heel on the snake just behind its head. And then—are you ready for this?—he reached down and picked it up. Right about where its neck would have been if it had had one.

"They'll need this at the hospital," he said, once the Spirit left him and he started speaking English again.

"It's a copperhead," I said. "They don't need it. Turn it loose."

Rick was brave up to this point. He had the faith to take up the serpent, but he didn't have any left to put it down with. He was scared to turn it loose, and I couldn't blame him.

By the time we got to the car, his leg had begun to swell, and he kept commenting—in the most colorful language—that I should get us to the emergency room as quickly as possible. He held the snake between his thumb and forefinger and extended his arm out the car window. Rick allowed the copperhead to dangle down toward the highway, its body swaying with the rushing wind. Two cars we met almost ran off the road, and a hitchhiker leapt into the ditch as we whizzed by. All of this occurred while we made the thirty-minute drive in half that time.

The waiting room was crowded. You'd be amazed at the influence of a three-foot copperhead dangling from the fist of a deranged man in a hospital emergency room. Several of the halt and lame were cured instantly. Some took up their beds and walked.

No wonder physicians use the caduceus as their symbol: two serpents entwined around a staff.

The receptionist was pecking away on a computer keyboard, oblivious to the commotion. Intent on her interrogation of a shirtless man with a bloody towel wrapped around his head, she had just finished asking him if he had ever had rheumatic fever, impetigo, or the measles, when she looked up. She yelled the international distress word, went crazy as a sprayed roach, and abandoned her post without being properly relieved.

The physician arrived within seconds, a young man, we learned later, who was from North Tonawanda, New York, interning in the Appalachian region amongst the aborigines of Middle Tennessee.

"It's a copperhead," I said, "and it bit him on the leg."

"If you knew what it was, why'd you bring it in here?"

"We wanted to make sure you knew," Rick said.

A few hours and some antivenom later, I drove Rick home where he continued his recuperation by forcing liquids until he fell asleep.

Months passed. After a first dusting of snow, Rick and I returned to the little creek where this saga begins.

We never found the pistol, although we searched for over an hour that dark, intimidating afternoon. Even though we never want to have that adventure again, the experience taught Rick and me a valuable lesson that all people should know. Human beings should always fear three things on this earth: snakes, sticks that look like snakes, and snakes that look like sticks.

Watch your step.

Marriage

I escaped matrimony for the first fifty-two years of my life, and then one day there she was. Her name is Kim, and she has taught me many things during this spell of marriage. Being married is not all that bad, but I've learned that it's like having company that never goes home. That reality is probably far more difficult for her than it ever is for me. Bless her heart.

We weren't married long until I discovered her hatred and fear of insects and rodents. I was soon to learn that she had appointed me to be our exterminator. I would hear her yell from upstairs: "Get up here quick. Something needs killing." Or she might scream, "Come here and see what the cat has cornered." She even called me at work one day to come home and step on a spider that invaded the kitchen. I did as I was ordered, but I reminded her of my own major fear.

Growing up in the country, I learned a lot about snakes, mainly to loathe them, but also that they sometimes travel in pairs or squads. I made clear to Kim my number one rule: "If you ever find a snake in this house, don't call me. Just burn it down, snake and all, and leave. It has a mate or some buddies in here somewhere. Just imagine two weeks later me opening my underwear drawer, reaching in and pulling out a writhing copperhead hissing in my face."

Kim may be afraid of harmless insects, but I can't understand why she isn't scared of things I won't go near. If they let her, she would drive in the Daytona 500 tomorrow. She also plans to parachute from a plane on her next birthday. I've tried to talk her out of it, but all is vanity. She'd gladly board the Mars Spaceship, the Space Shuttle, or any other craft that astronauts have spent years preparing for. Right now, though, she settles for rides at the county fair like the roller coaster and the double Ferris wheel. I wouldn't ride either of them with Marylin Monroe. Her favorite pastime, however, is bungee jumping, something she has attempted to get me to do for years. As one who loves my life, however, I have always declined.

A while back, she and I were driving down to Florida for a few days of vacation. I knew we'd have to argue about parasailing although our decisions were already made. She would fly, and I would stand on the beach and wave at her as she glided by. Shortly before we reached the Georgia state line, a billboard caught our attention. It said that if we turned off the interstate at the next exit, we could experience the South's tallest bungee tower. I knew then that I was in trouble. Before I could think of any excuse to keep going straight past it, Kim said, "Oh darling, can we please go there? I promise you'll love it."

"I've told you a hundred times," I said. "I don't ride rides, especially those high up in the sky that drop you to the ground with a piece of elastic or a Sans-a-Belt waist band wrapped around your ankle."

"Randy Cross, do you not know that all people should bungee jump at least one time in their lives?"

"Yes, I know that and have lived up to that decree. I've bungee jumped once, and that was at birth." Bless her heart, she was still laughing as we sped by the exit.

During the first few years of our marriage, Kim had still not developed the extraordinary skills as a chef she has now. She would attempt to cook, and I would attempt to eat it. Oh, it wasn't as bad as the dog let on. Being a Southern dog, he would eat the cornbread and little of anything else. He'd scour the neighborhood for scraps and unguarded pet food bowls. Every couple of weeks, he checked himself in at the animal shelter to get nutrition and gain a few pounds.

Speaking of dogs, there's a man in our neighborhood, and every afternoon between four-thirty and five he goes walking by our house leading one of these big topiary poodles. It looks like it's been carved up like an eighteenth-century English hedgerow. He's shaved off up to about his elbows and looks as though he has a fuzzy commode cover draped over his withers. His rear is bare, and there's a furry rug growing up each leg. His tail is shaved, and there's a poofy ball on the end. Between its ears is a little tuft of hair with a pink bow attached to it.

That grown man walks that dog out on the streets. My wife won't let me accost him, but I want to ask him as he walks by: "Have you no shame? Have you no dignity? Have you no manliness?" I'll bet his wife makes him, but I wouldn't do it. I'd rather trade wives than lead a topiary poodle out in public.

Language: Ain't It Something?

I have a wonderful hobby and a terrible curse that led to the same end. I think it's a good idea to let you know, since you are reading these pages, that I am a stickler for words. To paraphrase Mark Twain, he declared that the difference between the right word and the almost right word is the difference between lightning and the lightning bug. I stay tore up constantly with the television, radio, and printed sources.

I once wrote to a sauce company because the label had misused the word "its." The manufacturer declared that "it's" flavor was derived from a blend of spices. The sentence went something like this: The sauce is delicious because of the use of it's spices. The word "it's" means "it is." If this is true, and it is, their sentence really says: "The sauce is delicious because of it is spices." The label should have contained the word "its," not the contraction "it's." I wrote a letter to the company pointing out the grammatical error.

I received a note of thanks in return saying they'd correct the mistake on the label, but it didn't even contain a quarter-off coupon for my next purchase. That was all right. Please notice the words "all right."

The word "alright" does not exist. When it's used, it sounds alright, but it doesn't look all right. Never use "alright" again. All right?

Some years ago, our leaders here in Decatur, Alabama, decided to construct a new 20-million-dollar jail. That's not what we ended up with. Instead of a jail, we have a "correctional facility." The old building, now deserted, sits across the street with the memory of these penurious and pitiful words still lettered across the front: "Morgan County Jail," as precise a name as the commissioners could come up with, bless their hearts, a few decades ago when it was built. But that was back when a syllable was still worth a syllable. I'll bet it never occurred to them to call it anything but a jail, it being a jail and all—and jail being the perfect English word for such a place for over 500 years. We traded one good syllable for, let's see, "cor-rec-tion-al fa-cil-i-ty," eight bad ones.

I prefer the old word, the one we still use—at least for now—in various forms: jailbait, jailbird, jailbreak, jailhouse, and jailer. I don't guess we have a jailer anymore. That would not be possible without a jail. I suppose he is a correctional facilitator.

If this new multi-syllabic nomenclature catches on—as it is sure to do in a world that traded graveyard (two syllables) for cemetery (four), and cemetery for memorial gardens (six), imagine how devastating it will be to, if to nothing else, country music: "I'm stuck in jail, and you won't even go my bail." What if this linguistic lavishness had struck years ago? I offer three examples for you to contemplate the rest of the day: Dr. King's "Letter from Birmingham Jail," Elvis's "Jailhouse Rock," and Monopoly's "Go directly to Jail." Make the syllabic substitutions yourself. They hurt your brain, don't they?

And think about what this language inflation is doing to our youth. When our son was in the third grade, I picked him up from school one afternoon. When we were leaving the campus, I asked him what he had for lunch.

"Pizza. It was awesome."

"No," I said. "The Resurrection was awesome. Pizza is good."

A few days later, I picked him up again, and being an avid eater myself I asked again what he had for lunch. "They brought in chicken sandwiches from a restaurant," he said.

"How much did they cost?" I asked.

"Three dollars," he said.

Knowing that he didn't carry money to school, I asked him where he got it.

"From some dude," he said. I pulled the car over to the curb and stopped. "We don't have dudes at our house, and we certainly don't borrow money from them. What was the dude's name?"

"Sammy," he said.

Taking out my billfold, I retrieved three one-dollar bills. "Give these to Sammy first thing in the morning when you get to school, don't borrow money, and don't ever call anyone a dude." I have never heard him use the words "awesome" nor "dude" again.

Another linguistic incident occurred I want you to know about. Sammy and his family live near us, and the boys visit each other often. One day when they were playing in our yard, our son asked me this question: "May me'n Sammy have some ice cream?"

In response, I said "Sammy, have you been mean here in the yard? If so, you can't have any ice cream, and you'll have to go home."

Our son jumped in. "Sammy's not mean. He's always nice and easy to get along with. I'm sorry I called him mean. May Sammy and I have some ice cream?"

I took the apology and explained how good grammar can ensure that people convey their true intent. The boys enjoyed several helpings of ice cream that afternoon, and Sammy didn't go home until his normal time. Sometimes I believe it's more difficult to be the child of an English teacher than it is to be the child of a preacher.

It is no wonder teenagers inflate language.

They've grown up listening to TV commercials for car dealers: screaming announcers who shout about "extravaganzas" and "super mega blowout sales."

As the years slide by, people of all ages do their parts to weaken the language. A young man who took our order in a restaurant a while back introduced himself and said he would be our "wait person." Of course, I knew he was a waiter—just as I knew he was a person—so I didn't say anything to him about it. I'm sure it was not his fault. Somebody in a corporate office somewhere probably uses words like "proactive" instead of "active" and the word "impact" when he means "affect" or "influence." He could be one of the people who decided that "sales associate" was superior to "clerk."

If you are reading this sermon, please never use the word "plethora" in the place of "much" or "many." And I beg you: never use the three-syllable word "utilize" instead of the one-syllable word "use." Please notice the difference. "I utilize the lawn mower to mow the grass." "I use the lawn mower to mow the grass." You might even prefer "I mow the grass with a lawn mower."

This is an easy one. Never use "utilize." Always use "use" instead.

Searching for Richard Llewellyn

The novel *How Green Was My Valley* by Richard Llewellyn is the most beautiful, touching book I have ever read. When I finished it, I knew I would look at the world differently, forever. Mr. Llewellyn died on November 30, 1983, in Dublin, Ireland, but his body was returned for burial to the mining region of Wales, the setting for his heartbreaking lovely story.

Over the years, I have recommended *How Green Was My Valley* to hundreds of people, including my friends and students. None has loved it as much as my wife Kim. In her personal copy, she has a blue headscarf folded and draped over the front cover. When she needs to cry, she removes the scarf her late mother wore when she cleaned the house. After wrapping the cloth tightly around her hand, she then reads aloud the opening passage of the book, which recounts a scene of the author saying farewell to his childhood world. She knows that the poignant story is ours, everybody's. We have spent many evenings reading passages aloud to one another, wiping our eyes, and shaking our heads. "How does he do that?" we say. "How does he make such magic?"

One night we decided what we would do: Go to

Wales and place flowers on Richard Llewellyn's grave. We wanted to stand there beside him and tell him how his thoughts have moved us and then read him a few passages from his own words.

We opened a special savings account and added to it as we could: ten or twenty dollars here and there, maybe a hundred on a good month. After saving up for airline tickets, hotels, food, and a rental car, we went. We flew into London where we rented a green Citroen that took us on one of the most fascinating journeys we had ever made. There at the airport's gift shop we bought a bouquet of flowers and placed them in the back seat to have them ready when the time came.

After we drove into Wales, we stopped first at a tourist information center in Cardiff. The lovely smiling woman behind the counter spoke music to our Alabama ears. "Oh my dears, welcome to both of you. May I be of some assistance?"

"Yes, ma'am, could you direct us to the gravesite of Mr. Richard Llewellyn?"

"Oh my," the polite lady said. "I'm afraid I don't know. I do know that he lived in St. David's up on the coast. Let me call there." The St. David's lady had no idea, but she suggested we call the Center for British Historic Preservation in London. The woman there apologized for not knowing—said she ought to know—but give her a few days to research it.

Through the breathtaking countryside we drove, passing large green road signs written in the impossible language of the Welsh, with English subtitles. We stopped at every Tourist Information Office we came to. No luck. A lady in Cardigan thought she had the answer: call the Chairman of the Welsh Department at the University of Wales. Kim and I thought that sounded right. After all, *How Green Was My Valley* is the most famous Welsh novel ever written. She called him. "This is Professor Williams," she whispered, handing me the phone.

"Professor," I said, "can you direct me to the gravesite of Mr. Richard Llewellyn?"

"Oh dear. I'm afraid I can't. I'm relatively certain that he is dead, but I do not know where he is interred." I thanked him and hung up.

"Let's just drive," I said to Kim. "We'll find that good man yet." We drove for days, our little green car whizzing along motorways, creeping over sheep-infested gravel roads bordered by ancient rock fences. And then, there it was, an imposing group of stone buildings just off the highway: "The Center for the Cultural Preservation of Wales." Signs directed us up a cobbled road to the administration building that bespoke learning, erudition, and Richard Llewellyn's grave.

"May I help you?" a polite lady inquired.

"Yes, ma'am," I said. "Is there somebody—anybody—who can direct us to the grave of Wales' most famous novelist, Mr. Richard Llewellyn?"

"Of course," she said. "We have several here who can."

"Could you show us to one of those offices?"

"Oh, no," she said. "They're all academics."

"I can talk with academics," I said. "I come from the University of Mississippi."

"Oh, I'm afraid that's not possible. Perhaps I could telephone one for you."

Kim and I agreed that would be fine.

"Yes, sir," I said. "Could you tell me where Richard Llewellyn is buried?"

"Oh, dear, I'm afraid I don't know."

"If you come to America," I said, "I will be pleased to take you to the graves of Mark Twain, William Faulkner, and Ernest Hemingway. All of them. We keep up with our dead writers."

That afternoon, I called London once again and spoke with the woman who had promised to research the issue. "Oh, Mr. Cross," the woman said. "Our staff have been discussing your situation, and we have decided that Mr. Llewellyn was cremated, his ashes strewn throughout the Welsh mining country. Perhaps you have driven through him several times. That's the best we can suppose."

We stopped the car near Tregaron with the remains of a coal mine visible in the distance. We placed the bouquet of flowers a few feet into the woods, retrieved the book from the back seat, and together read aloud the last sentence from one of the most extraordinary novels ever created. Then, Kim and I recited the words we had written during our drive early that morning. "God bless you, Richard Llewellyn, wherever you may be."

Ruby

Have you ever owned an inanimate object you couldn't stand to get rid of? Loving it as though it were human? Some people call that affliction "anthropomorphism," but that's too much word for me. Besides, if I used it, people might expect me to say words like "plethora," "proactive," "awesome," and "iconic," which of course I never would. How do we come to think of objects, even pets, as people? Don't get me started on the phrase "pet parents." My wife and I have two tolerable cats, but we are not their parents. If we were, we could go with the circus.

Have you ever put a Santa Claus hat on a cat or a Roll Tide sweater on a Yorkie? Some people in our neighborhood found a small houndstooth hat they attached to the head of their boa constrictor with a rubber band. That is wrong in all the ways a thing can be wrong. That's anthropomorphism the best I can tell, and I'm against it. At least I was.

In 1998, I bought a new red Buick I named Ruby. We were together for fourteen years. That's seventy in human years, according to one automobile expert. She never let me down, not once in the 238,000 miles we travelled together, the equivalent of nearly ten trips around the Equator.

One night late, Ruby and I were on our way home from Huntsville in a rainstorm. Halfway to Decatur she lost power, but she didn't quit running. She just sort of sunk down, her speed dropping from sixty to thirty. I said, "Come on, Ruby, you've got to get us home." I patted the dashboard on her favorite spot. We made it. Before I got out, I thanked her for being a loyal friend. "You're a good girl, Rube," I said. The next day, when the mechanic told me he didn't know how the motor had kept running, I wanted to say, "She's too faithful to strand me on a stormy night," but I was afraid he would accuse me of anthropomorphism.

Several months ago, my wife Kim and I drove Ruby to Birmingham and abandoned her among hundreds of cars she had never seen before. With tears we attempted to conceal from the salesman, we drove out of the lot in our new car. "Don't look back," she said, like I might have been Lot's wife. A couple of weeks later, I found Ruby's spare key in my billfold. "Throw it away," Kim said. I didn't want to, but she made me, like a mother makes a child give up his blanket. The sight of that key brought to my mind journeys we had made, places we had been, vacations, weddings, funerals, and hundreds of trips to Lucky's Supermarket.

Occasionally I see cars that look like Ruby, and my heart leaps up like Wordsworth's when he saw the rainbow. I know it's not right for me to feel this way, but I can't help it. Even so, I would never attempt to put Alabama sweaters on the cats as though they were our children. Besides, they wouldn't tolerate it if I tried. They both pull for Ole Miss.

Sign of the Times

One summer day in 1962, my friends Ronnie Springer and Ray Farris and I were sitting on the porch of Raleigh Green's store in St. Joseph, Tennessee. The oak bench, reserved for grown-ups, was occupied that day by Mose Creel, Clinton Roberson, and Bluford Bradley. Clinton was telling a story about traveling with the World of Pleasure Shows—we called it the fair—when Clem Cross came hurrying down the hill.

"They've just put up a stop sign down by the bank," Clem said.

"Aye Gunnies, I got to see this," Clinton said, standing up, folding his knife, and brushing the cedar shavings from his lap. Before he stepped off the porch, Ronnie, Ray, and I jumped on our bicycles and tore out, eager to see.

Clem had not exaggerated. There it stood: a sure-enough stop sign like they had up in Lawrenceburg and down in Florence. It was attached to a rusted metal post, one corner curled like the lid of a sardine can. It was used.

We parked our bicycles across the road in Mrs. Mable Moore's front yard and sat on the ground, enthralled, watching the show. Other boys joined us as well as a few men. "Reckon how we come to get that?" Miley Haygood said.

"Marvin Bryan owns the bank, and he's a state senator," Red Black told him. "He's got a lot of power up there in Nashville."

Cars began to line up on the street, sometimes backed up even to the post office. A car would pull up to the sign, stop, and then ease on off. Whenever a person stayed stopped too long, hogging the sign, other drivers tapped their horns. Several circled the block and got back in line so they could stop again.

When we got back to Mr. Green's store, Clem was still talking. "They tell me," he said, "that that sign come from Nashville, close to the Grand Ole Opry."

"Law," said Mose Creel, "I bet Hank Williams stopped at that sign a bunch of times, Minnie Pearl, too."

"Aye Gunnies," Clinton said. "I'll tell you a nuthern—Kitty Wells. Ain't she a honky tonk angel?" The men all laughed and agreed that she was.

They talked along and speculated, bringing up the names of other luminaries who had stopped at our sign in Cadillacs and Lincolns on their way to the Ryman Auditorium.

I was in St. Joe last weekend. Mr. Green's store is gone, like the men who once gathered on its porch to talk and whittle. Ronnie and Ray gone, too, the old bank now a Senior Citizens Center. There beside it, its rusted post tilted, is the faded sign, still on duty. I drove up to it and stopped. No one was behind me, so I sat there far longer than my turn. Then, I circled the block and came back around, one more time.

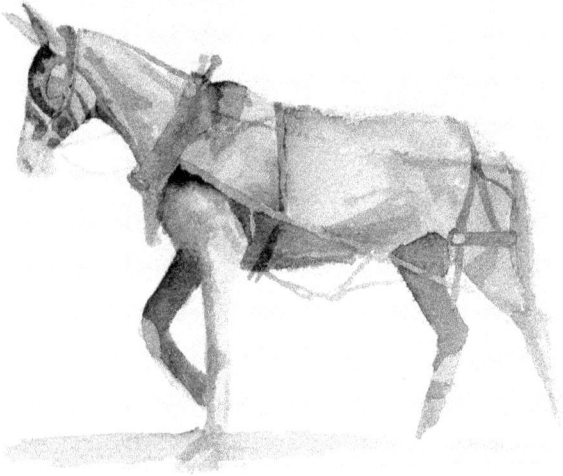

Through Old Ground

Mr. Andy Landers' entrance into town was always the same. Town, for Mr. Landers and the rest of us living in St. Joseph, Tennessee, in the 1950s, was Raleigh Green's grocery store just across the road from our house. He didn't own a car, so he traveled wherever he went by tractor—a once-red Farmall "A" bleached pink by too many years in the Tennessee sun. It suited Andy Landers. We could see him every day, about an hour after dinner, as he topped the hill where the L&N switch track crossed the road: Mr. Landers sitting solemn in the seat, Trigger and Old Eller fully harnessed and tied loose-reined behind the tractor's drawbar hitch. He always brought his mules to rent to people in town who had no other way to plow their gardens. But he wouldn't rent to just anybody.

My father was one of his regular renters. Daddy used Old Eller throughout the spring and summer to break, cultivate, and finally lay by the field behind our house. "Nothing," Daddy would say, "plows as good as a mule, and I never saw a better one than Old Eller. She understands more about making a crop than most men I know."

Daddy plowed, and I walked alongside and listened to the ringing of the trace chains, the pleasant squeak of leather against leather and hame against collar. Over all these sounds were Old Eller's steady breathing and Daddy's gentle instructions to her: "whoap," "haw back," "come up," "gee," "haw now," the cotton lines draped around his waist.

After half an hour or so, Mr. Landers always crossed the road from the store with something in his hand. All three of us knew what: a Pay Day candy bar for Old Eller. Daddy unhitched the plow and the single tree from the traces and guided Old Eller to the shade of the white oak at the south end of the field. By the time he removed the bridle, Mr. Landers would be there saying quietly, almost apologetically, what he always said: "Old Eller's old like me, and she gets tired." Then he unwrapped the candy and offered it to her in one piece on the flat of his palm. The long green- and brown-stained teeth would chew, and the thick tongue and lips would smack at the sticky, sugary caramel. Through it all, Mr. Landers stood silent, stroking Old Eller's sweat-darkened neck with the back of his fingers.

Years later, at Mr. Landers' funeral, the undertakers placed green pine branches on top of his casket once it was lowered into the grave. Malcolm, Mr. Landers' son, explained why. "Daddy wanted us to do it," he said, "so Mama wouldn't have to hear the dirt hit the top of the coffin."

I don't think Mr. Landers ever knew my name. I was just a little boy walking beside his daddy and Old Eller in the field. But even now, the memory of those days sometimes eases through my mind like a good, slow mule pulling a turning plow through old ground.

"It surely is a strange thing how incidents, trifles in themselves, penetrate one's life and grow and grow and change its whole pattern, while other matters of apparent great import fade into nothing."

From *Laughing Stock*, the posthumous autobiography of T. S. Stribling. Edited by Randy K. Cross and John T. McMillan. Published by the University of Alabama Press

Acknowledgements

I could never have completed this book alone. The publisher, Angela Broyles, encouraged me throughout this endeavor. My dear friend, Brooke Alexander, produced beautiful and talented pieces of art that illustrate the writing. The fine computer technology came about thanks to the skill of my brother-in-law, Richard Sims. My sweet wife, Kimberly, kept the project going and offered outstanding suggestions as the editor.

I am honored to be associated for many years with Calhoun Community College. The administrators, staff, and my colleagues provided an extraordinary place to work. The students in my classes made me eager to attend. I still recall us learning and laughing. I thank you.

www.ingramcontent.com/pod-product-compliance
Lightning Source LLC
Chambersburg PA
CBHW041254160426
42812CB00084B/2498